J Two Guides for the ourney

Two Guides for the Journey

Thomas Aquinas and William Langland on the Virtues

Sheryl Overmyer

CASCADE *Books* • Eugene, Oregon

TWO GUIDES FOR THE JOURNEY
Thomas Aquinas and William Langland on the Virtues

Copyright © 2016 Sheryl Overmyer. All rights reserved. Except for brief quotations in critical publications or reviews, no part of this book may be reproduced in any manner without prior written permission from the publisher. Write: Permissions, Wipf and Stock Publishers, 199 W. 8th Ave., Suite 3, Eugene, OR 97401.

Cascade Books
An Imprint of Wipf and Stock Publishers
199 W. 8th Ave., Suite 3
Eugene, OR 97401

www.wipfandstock.com

PAPERBACK ISBN: 978-1-4982-2899-2
HARDCOVER ISBN: 978-1-4982-2901-2
EBOOK ISBN: 978-1-4982-2900-5

Cataloguing-in-Publication data:

Names: Overmyer, Sheryl.
Title: Two guides for the journey : Thomas Aquinas and William Langland on the virtues / Sheryl Overmyer.
Description: Eugene, OR : Cascade Books, 2016 | Includes bibliographical references and index.
Identifiers: ISBN 978-1-4982-2899-2 (paperback) | ISBN 978-1-4982-2901-2 (hardcover) | ISBN 978-1-4982-2900-5 (ebook)
Subjects: LCSH: Virtues. | Thomas, Aquinas, Saint, 1225?–1274. | Langland, William, 1330?–1400? Piers Plowman.
Classification: BJ1521 .O84 2016 (print) | BJ1521 .O84 (ebook)

Manufactured in the U.S.A.   OCTOBER 26, 2016

An earlier version of chapter 1 was published as "Three More Jigs in the Puzzle: The Unity of Analogy, Beatitude and Virtue in Thomas' Summa Theologiae," International Journal of Systematic Theology 15 (2013) 374–93, and is reprinted with permission.

To my teachers

Contents

Acknowledgments | ix

Introduction | 1

1 A Roadmap | 11
  §1 *The Unity of Analogy, Beatitude, and Virtue* | 12
  §2 *A Primer on Analogy* | 14
  §3 *Beatitude: Aristotelian Beginning, Supernatural End* | 18
  §4 *Virtues' Various Ends* | 23
  §5 *A Glimpse of Our Ultimate End in Christ* | 30

2 Will's Wanderings | 35
  §1 *Lost in Meed* | 36
    1.1 *Meed's (Im)Morality* | 39
    1.2 *Losing Law, Love, and Virtue* | 46
  §2 *Between Meed and Charity* | 56

3 The Way of Charity | 60
  §1 *These Three Remain: Faith, Hope, and . . .* | 61
  §2 *Charity Embodied* | 66
  §3 *Charity's Community* | 71
  §4 *Conclusion Mid-Way* | 75

4 Surprises Along the Way | 78
  §1 *The Acquired and Infused Virtues* | 79
  §2 *The "Acquired" Infused Virtues* | 81
  §3 *The "Infused" Acquired Virtues* | 90

5   Help and Obstacles Along the Way | 95
        §1 *Grace Gave the Cardinal Virtues* | 98
        §2 *Come Again?* | 106
        §3 *Learn to Love* | 112

    Epilogue: Our Two Guides | 118

    Appendix: Summary of the Action of Piers Plowman | 119
    Bibliography | 125
    Subject Index | 137

Acknowledgments

I HAVE BEEN BLESSED with the best teachers, each of whom—curiously like the saints—differ from one another as night to day. I began to write this book as a dissertation under the supervision of Stanley Hauerwas, David Aers, Paul Griffiths, and Amy Laura Hall. I sought out these mentors guided by David Burrell, David Solomon, and Alasdair MacIntyre. I found my way to them through the advice of Alfred Freddoso. And I landed upon this advisor, in some way or another, from advice given by Stephanie and Thomas Nevins—my sister and brother-in-law.

The experience of learning what my teachers had to teach was so formative that I cannot identify portions of my writing that are untouched by fellow students, including Ben Dillon, Joel Halldorf, and Matthew Whelan. Joe Wiebe, who descends from Mennonite royalty, remains the crème de la crème. Sean Larsen always has something to add, and he added much that is worthwhile to this book. How I would have survived without the two persons of Natalie Carnes and Greg Lee remains a mystery. I have the best of friends in Rachael Deagman, who is good and good at everything she does.

DePaul University gave me a job and continues to support my research, putting me ever further in its debt. Its extra support during the summer of 2011, in the form of a Faculty Research and Development Grant, was crucial. The fellow faculty of the Department of Catholic Studies has been like a family. During these crucial revision periods, Kate Crassons' critical and charitable readings were a great gift.

I am thrilled that my first book is ushered in by Wipf and Stock Publishers. They print many of my teachers' books, and now lend paper and ink to this student's fruits. They harness the printed word to create colleagues and community. To its editors and readers, I am grateful.

Introduction

ALONG THE JOURNEY OF our life, we are hard-pressed to find more excellent guides in the way of virtue than Thomas Aquinas and William Langland. These two medieval Christians inherited the dynamic metaphor of journeying as a fundamental concept of the Christian life and harnessed it to animate their magisterial texts: the *Summa Theologiae* and *Piers Plowman*.[1] Christians' journey back to God consists in the way of charity, yet it is far from straightforward or sequential. Rather, it is impinged upon by epistemic ambiguity, our willful continued habits of resistance, and inherent limitations on our perfection. The virtues are divine gifts humanly received, *treasure in earthen vessels* (2 Cor 4:7).

In this book, Thomas' writing on the virtues illustrates two features of the moral life that mutually condition one another: (1) every trace of human virtue is a participation in God, and there is no virtue that is not subject to voracious theological logic. To this end, Thomas develops categorizations of the virtues—whether moral and theological virtue; acquired and infused virtue; false, imperfect, and perfect virtue—to differentiate the intensity of our participation in ultimate goodness. The second feature, (2), is that there is always room for growth and progress in the moral life. Even

---

1. I use the standard English translation of the *Summa Theologiae* by the Fathers of the English Dominican Province cross-referenced with the Leonine edition—*Opera omnia* (edited by Roberto Busa from the Leonine edition; adapted by Enrique Alarcón), available via http://www.corpusthomisticum.org—and Alfred Freddoso's new English translation, *Summa Theologiae*. I will use George Economou's translation of the C-version: William Langland, *Piers Plowman; A Verse Translation*. When relevant, in the footnotes I note differences in George Russell and George Kane's edition, *Piers Plowman: The C Version*, alongside Derek Pearsall's 2nd edition, *Piers Plowman: An Edition of the C-Text*. Note that Economou's verse translation is tied to Pearsall's 1978 edition, so there are systematic differences in line numbers and text.

1

the perfect may progress. Thomas communicates this qualification even as he writes about the most perfect of virtues, charity. In sum, these two features provide us wayfarers dual assurance that we are indeed on the way back to God, and that our journey is far from complete. Thomas brings to Langland an orderly moral framework, and his confidence in the work of grace can help us envisage an extension of Easter joy into all liturgical time.

Filling out this picture of the virtues, Langland's writing displays the messiness of our attempts to make progress back to God. The moral life defies neatly ordered progress because the institutions and practices meant to sustain the virtues instead undermine them. We who are on the way are embodied, wounded creatures. These are the virtues as practiced under the conditions of late medieval culture, with added layers of complexity in their existential, social, political, and institutional aspects. Langland is particularly concerned with our habituation to sin and to this end, affords a special light on the underbelly of the moral life: how a culture marred by vice produces individuals whose nature is transformed by sin such that they willingly cut themselves off from grace of the sacraments borne in virtue, and how such individuals call themselves Christians. Langland brings a narratival complexity and imagination to Thomas' treatment of the virtues. The poem itself even embodies this experience through its recursiveness and repetition.

Reading them together, the *Summa* and *Piers* generate a picture of virtue that accounts for an ideal while attending to the reality of our embodied, fallen existence. The *Summa* and *Piers* point to unqualifiedly perfect virtue—true virtue given by Christ, sustained in the sacraments, and nurtured by the community of the church. Yet these are not the only practices or only communities that shape us, for sin and vice bear too much reality. The virtues we attain in this life are formed and deformed by grace and sin. The virtues are shaped by us, others, sin, sacraments, the church; the virtues are also shaped by corrupting practices and outside institutions. To wit, reading these authors together show the complexity we ourselves will find along this journey, enable our understanding to appreciate that complexity, and in limited ways cultivate the virtues they describe.

What remains for us wayfarers is growth in Christ's charity, to "learn to love," which is all that matters (XXII.208). Yet even as one is graced with the most perfect of virtues, Langland demonstrates the vulnerability of such perfection and Thomas builds into charity a sense of incompletion and relative qualification. At the same time as Langland and Thomas chart

INTRODUCTION

our possibilities for perfection, they mark the reality of our imperfection—our epistemic ambiguity, our continued habits of resistance, and our inherent limitations on perfection in this life. For us there is no final static goal, no resting, no ceasing to progress along the way—in this life.

Our New Guide: Langland

This book focuses on the virtues treated side by side in the *Summa* and *Piers*. Given the history of interpretation of each medieval text and the modern disciplines that typically focus on each, the book will likely be of most interest to Thomists and scholars of the virtue ethics tradition. It may also be of interest to Langland scholars interested in a theological reading of the poem. I hope the latter will increasingly be the case as more scholars devote themselves to Langland's mature version of the poem, the C-version. Because my anticipated audience of Christian theologians is more likely familiar with Thomas and less likely familiar with Langland, I should say more about *Piers* as a fourteenth-century poem, the action of the poem, and its reception history.

Piers Plowman is the sole lifelong work of William Langland. There are fifty-some surviving manuscripts in the hand of his near-contemporaries, and based on a similar number of manuscripts of Geoffrey Chaucer's *Canterbury Tales*, it should impress readers that their renown in their own time was comparable. Langland's manuscripts give evidence of three distinct versions: the A-version, written in the 1360s; the B-version as an augmentation of the A-version, in the 1370s; and the C-version as the result of a number of additions, deletions, and shifts in the 1380s. Immediately the poem assumed a culturally prominent role. It was cited by John Bell during the English Rising (Peasant's Revolt) of 1381 and in the sixteenth-century, it was taken into the hands of ecclesial reformers who read it as a proto-Protestant text.

Piers bears traces of Langland's impressive erudition in his drawing upon Holy Scripture, commentaries, florilegia, Augustine, twelfth-century monastic sources, and divine liturgy. It gives ample evidence of Langland's contemporary realities of living in the aftermath of the Black Death and the Great Schism, amid succeeding plagues and clarion and competing calls for ecclesial reform, and growing labor disputes. The poem is Langland's achievement of bringing his command of the Catholic tradition to bear on the new moral challenges it faces in the late medieval period—to scrutinize the fourteenth-century church and its sacramental culture, social fragmentation, corrupted and corrupting political institutions, and the emerging market economy. The final result is a theological allegorical dream vision of tradition-informed imagination.

Piers Plowman is written with a Prologue and twenty-two Passus (Steps). The plot of *Piers* is difficult to trace. From the beginning, the poem's narrative follows a wanderer, an allegorical personification we discover is named Will, who first undertakes a quest to hear wonders. Through the processes of this complex poem, Will's desire is reoriented toward God. The process of conversion is complicated and in every aspect, the poem's contours are challenging to limn: its figures as allegorical personifications are seldom clearly delineated and often changing, its themes are mingled in models that are either adopted or further developed or set aside, and the meanings of the poem are embedded in multiple strands of thought that are sometimes woven tightly together and other times loosely strung throughout. In this book, I focus on three episodes: Prologue–Passus V, XVIII–XIX, and XXI–XXII. These are Langland's most explicit and extended treatments of virtue. These prominent episodes on the fate of the virtues are mere signposts in view of the whole complex course of *Piers*.[2]

Thomists new to *Piers* are likely to wonder about existing Thomistic readings of the poem. To simplify matters: there are none of the C-version of the poem (i.e., the version of concern here) and little of the A- and B-versions. In Langland's own century and in the five centuries following, there are no known extended engagements of Langland by Thomists. During the twentieth century, a handful of Thomists touched upon early versions of the poem—the A-version or the B-version.[3] But I engage the theologically rich C-version. These three versions, the A-version, B-version, and C-version, were in circulation since Walter Skeat's editions of 1867, 1869, and 1873. But since the publication of Derek Pearsall's magisterial C-version in 1978, "more and more of what is written about the poem takes [the C-version] into serious account even as some critics assert that they prefer to concentrate their reading on this third and final version because it offers the fullest expression of Langland's intellectual and spiritual development."[4] The truth

---

2. For a summary of the poem's action, consult my Appendix; Pearsall, "Introduction"; and Salter, "*Piers Plowman*: An Introduction."

3. Dunning, *Piers Plowman: An Interpretation of the A-Text*, and Morgan, "The Meaning of Kind Wit, Conscience, and Reason."

4. Economou, preface to *William Langland's Piers Plowman*, viii.

Introduction

of this observation is confirmed on a wide scale with George Russell and George Kane's edition of the C-version in 1997 and Pearsall's updated critical edition in 2008.

Langland studies are flourishing in the wake of Langland's mature theological forays disclosed in the C-version. Several Langland scholars interested in theology show us how to read *Piers* as a theological rather than secular poem.[5] Rather than treating Langland's theology and ecclesiology "as confused (or brilliant) anticipations of some contemporary and thoroughly secularized theoretical paradigm," these scholars place themselves in a longer standing tradition that asserts the validity of a diachronic theological reading of Christian conversation across centuries.[6] Not only is this mode of engagement a viable alternative to secular ones, it is characteristic of fourteenth-century Christians themselves.

In short, *Piers* is ripe for a theological reading centered on virtue. I engage the poem on this register, and go further in reading the poem as standing fully within the Christian virtue ethics tradition without traces of heterodoxy attributed to it.[7] This book is an invitation for theologians to take note so that they might consider expanding the canon to include the compelling, imaginative, and challenging moral vision of Langland.

Our Two Different Guides

This book conjoins the accounts of the virtues from *Summa* and *Piers* to produce a fuller overall picture of our life's journey. Using both Thomas and Langland, it charts every point of our moral possibilities—from sinner to saint—and follows us as we find our way between the two. Reading them side-by-side is no straightforward task because of the nature of the way

---

5. E.g., Aers, *Sanctifying Signs* and *Salvation and Sin*; Crassons, *The Claims of Poverty*; Davlin, *The Place of God*; Salter, "*Piers Plowman*: An Introduction."

6. Aers, *Sanctifying Signs*, ix–x; *Salvation and Sin*, xiii.

7. Cf. Piers' moral teaching as semi-Pelagian (Robert Adams and Vance Smith), legalistic (Patricia Kean), apocalyptic (Martin Bloomfield, Kathryn Kerby-Fulton), correlative of an idealized version of the church (Eamon Duffy), or "Augustinian" without reference to Augustine's Christology, Trinitarianism, or ecclesiology. All such readings distort the picture of the virtues differently—rendering them powers of our own willing (semi-Pelagian), superfluous to a proto-Kantian framework (legalistic), a vestige amongst the evils of the present (apocalyptic), divinizing powers (idealized), or shorn of their theological grounding ("Augustinian" without Christology, Trinitarianism, or ecclesiology). Aers, *Salvation and Sin*, 4.

of virtue itself. By turns, our Christian journey is helped by grace and the sacraments and hindered by our conformity to the world and continued habits of sin. This path looks less like a forward march and more like a loop from the confessional to the altar, out to the world, and back again.

For another reason, this is no straightforward task because of the different genres of texts that depict this journey. The *Summa* is a work of systematic moral theology, a beginner's manual for Dominicans in training, a display of dialectical modes of reasoning expressed scholastically.[8] *Piers* is a work of allegorical poetry, a series of dream visions, an arrangement of episodes dialectically ordered such that later episodes allow the reader to re-narrate earlier episodes to explain figures' failures and partial successes. Although both operate pedagogically and dialectically and theologically, their differences in genre mean that they operate pedagogically and dialectically and theologically *differently*.

Ludwig Wittgenstein offers a suggestive paradigm for reading the differences between the *Summa* and *Piers*. He writes,

> We speak of understanding a sentence in the sense in which it can be replaced by another which says the same; but also in the sense in which it cannot be replaced by any other. (Any more than one musical theme can be replaced by another.)
>
> In the one case the thought in the sentence is something common to different sentences; in the other, something that is expressed only by these words in these positions. (Understanding a poem.)[9]

In the one case, we understand in the sense that there is a thought "common to different sentences," achieved through any number of expressions. Words can be rearranged, substituted, paraphrased, or "replaced by another which says the same." All of this is possible without a loss of meaning. In the other case, we understand in the sense that there is a single thought inseparable from its specific expression, "expressed only by these words in these positions." Just as musical themes "cannot be replaced by any other," but require a specific arrangement of notes in a certain order, so too a poem's content is inseparable from its form. Any attempt at paraphrasing or substitution results in a loss of meaning. (One might call this the "soul" of poetry

---

8. For precedent reading the *Summa Theologiae* as a pedagogical text, see works by Boyle, MacIntyre, and Jordan.

9. Wittgenstein, *Philosophical Investigations*, §531; see §§532–33 (143–44).

in that its form is integral to its content.[10]) Wittgenstein uses this heuristic to identify a unified concept of understanding achieved differently by two genres—through prose statements and through poetry.

The *Summa* theorizes virtue in its prose whereas *Piers* is a theory through poetry. The *Summa* makes claims about the virtues through its statements whereas *Piers* attains to truth *qua* poetry. Therefore it is *Piers qua* poem, not *Piers* transposed into prose, that comes to us as Langland's viable theory of virtue.

This approach to *Piers* may sound odd because it depends upon a set of assumptions that are contrary to our culture's dominant ethos, namely that poetry itself may be true or false. Alasdair MacIntyre argues that the compartmentalizations of modern culture tempt us to think that questions of truth or falsity belong to the purview of the sciences and theoretical inquiry whereas poetry belongs to a different order altogether.[11] The idea is common enough that poetry is true or false insofar as one transposes it into a simple prose statement that says something true or false. But this would be to treat poetry as prose in transposing it, in translating its meaning, in theorizing about it.

Poetry attains to truth or falsity *qua* poetry. It does so by presenting us with "structures in which, although concepts and propositions may appear, they are subordinated to, and in key part derive their sense and significance from, images of greater or lesser complexity. It is in and through the image that poetic form and philosophical content are unified."[12] These images are true or false in what they show—images are true insofar as they are revelatory, false insofar as they obscure, disguise, or distort. In this, poetry works differently than prose. The images to which the structures of poetry are indebted are true or false in what they *show*, whereas prose statements are true or false in what they *say*. When one conjoins an image to others, it may either acquire new revelatory power or lose what it previously had. When one conjoins a statement to others, a true statement remains true regardless of the other statements.[13]

Accordingly, I write about the *Summa* and *Piers* differently. *Piers* presented the greatest challenge to me. I am most conscious that as one myself, what Thomists most want is to surrender the poem's understanding

---

10. Ibid., §530 (143).
11. MacIntyre, "Poetry as Political Philosophy," 146.
12. Ibid.
13. Ibid.

to Thomas' all-consuming synthesis—to rearrange the content of the poem to the ordering of the *Summa*, to re-describe the allegorical figures and concepts according to the *Summa's* authoritative categories, to submit the judgments arising from the poem's process to the *Summa's* final authority. It would be much easier to treat Langland as if his writing was Thomas'. Instead, I give space to the poetry to do its work. I present *Piers* by laying out extended quotes and minute particulars. This presentation enables readers to understand the poem itself—thoughts "expressed only by these words in these positions,"[14] "poetry *qua* poetry."[15]

Although reading and writing about the *Summa* forms the canon of Catholic moral theology, it is no less contentious—and for those who are members of the guild even more so. Unsurprisingly, Thomists are convinced that much if not everything Thomas says is true, but *which* true statements one conjoins determines the resulting image of the virtues. In writing about the virtues in the *Summa*, I took the wide view by setting out first with the *Prima Pars* and carrying over Thomas' insights into the virtues into the *Secunda* and *Tertia Pars*. This approach of reading the *Summa* as a whole, rather than segmented into its parts, is now commonly agreed as needful.[16] The result yields a different image of the virtues than conventionally portrayed. Precisely because of Thomas' preoccupation with God in the *Prima Pars* can Thomas articulate a way for all human virtue to refer to God in the subsequent parts. Here Thomas' vision of virtue is capacious precisely because it is thoroughly theological. Tethering the virtues to the Triune God becomes a logic for the real possibilities for our perfection *and* why, human as we insist on being, we continually come short of this ultimate goal.

Stages of the Journey

Chapter 1 sets the stage for the book by using the *Summa* to chart the whole of the moral life, beginning and ending with a single reality: God. These robust *Theo*-logical commitments give rise to a correspondingly theological account of the virtues. Thus we can lay hold of the whole range of possibilities for our moral perfection. It is all there, from beginning to end. Any progress in the moral life begins and ends with Christ.

14. Wittgenstein, *Philosophical Investigations*, §531, 143–44.
15. MacIntyre, "Poetry as Political Philosophy," 146.
16. It is becoming commonplace to accept that the *Summa* ought to be read as a whole in the decades since MacIntyre's *Three Rival Versions of Moral Enquiry*.

Introduction

This Thomistic account can seem to be a comprehensive and complete account of the moral life. Yet in turning to chapter 2 and *Piers Plowman*, we see the world from within the messy contingencies of lived existence. We begin with a wayfarer named Will. Searching for a guide or guidance, he depends on what comes most naturally and immediate in his worldly desires. He begins to make his way through a world also thoroughly assimilated to the practices of the market. These practices of exchange warp human relations and the community itself, such that the virtues are mere parodies, vitiated to their core. The law of the land, which is intended to serve the common good and order relationships in the community, instead serves the interests of the lawmakers. This episode (Passus I-IV) is a critique of "virtue" and "law" as (de)formed by the economy and practices of exchange.

From within *this* moral landscape, messy as it is, Will is utterly lost. Chapter 3 takes up an episode much later in Will's quest (Passus XVIII–XIX) when the ultimate answer to his search for salvation is finally disclosed in a retelling of the Parable of the Good Samaritan. Langland allegorizes the relationship between sin and salvation as it relates to conversion and the church. We glimpse the form of decidedly christological virtue, a true community founded on Christ, and the healing practices of the sacraments. Here, much like at the end of chapter 1, we have the fullest, most complete meaning of "virtue." Even though Will learns that he cannot save his own soul, but rather he must depend on the sacramental resources of the church, he still struggles with discerning the way. Ultimately, the poem affirms the absolute priority of charity in the moral life alongside the limits of our ability to embody it.

Chapter 4 sustains and extends this focus on charity, delving deeper into Thomas' treatment of charity. Even in this most perfect virtue, Thomas tells us that we remain incomplete. Even the greatest perfection in this life is relative to perfection possible in the next. Perfection in this life is not and cannot be a static final goal at which some have already arrived. We are an incomplete work. For Thomas, all human virtue points us toward a single destiny: God; all human virtue is perfected in one person: Christ.

In chapter 5, I conclude with the ending of *Piers*. The ending of the poem articulates a concern that demands our sustained attention alongside our categorical need for Christ, the Church, and sacraments: our habituation to sin. Upon the wake of Thomas' sustained treatment of the virtues, Langland offers a sustained meditation on sin's effect on virtue, sacramental practice, relations in the community, and the Church. He tends to the distortion of sin wrought on the infused moral virtues, the blinded pragmatism of individuals who forego the sacramental-moral life for their familiar vicious habits, and the devastating effects of this rejection of the sacraments upon the community. This last chapter uses Langland to disclose the power of sin, emphasizing all the more the priority of Christ. In the end, the only thing that matters for the *Summa* and *Piers* is the consummation of charity: learning to love as Christ loves us.

1

A Roadmap

Beatitude is our destiny, our final goal. It is that which the wanderer Will seeks. It is that which we all seek. Thomas' account of beatitude stands prominently at the outset of the *Prima Secundae* and any proper introduction to Thomas' moral vision begins on this note. Yet this "note" is more akin to a characteristic mark that leaves an imprint on the whole of Thomas' teaching. In fact, the entire *Summa* holds at its forefront the ultimate end of our journey as beatitude. The Prologues of its parts tell the whole story: The *Prima Pars* leads with God, who is both Beatitude and Virtue in Godself; The *Secunda Pars* describes the human movement toward God, where beatitude and virtue derive from God; and The *Tertia Pars* gives us Christ as our way of going to God, whose perfection returns us to where we began in God. In this chapter, I regard the *Summa* as a roadmap for the course of human life.

The quintessential trail markers of this roadmap are Thomas' variations on *via* (journey)—we are *viatores* (wayfarers), on the *via salutis* (way of salvation), whose recourse is *viaticum* (the sacraments), given and sustained by the *Via* (Christ). Thus the virtues find their origin and end in this arc—the virtues are gifts given to us wayfarers by Christ, sustained in the sacraments, that we might make progress along the way of salvation.[1] In this life, the sense of being on-the-way is inexorable. As perfect as our virtues may become now, there is always room for virtues' increase. They

---

1. Aquinas, *Summa Theologiae*, 1.2.Prologue; 3.3.Prologue. See also Torrell, *Saint Thomas Aquinas*, vol. 2, esp. 69–75. Thomas demonstrates a masterful facility with language as he delineates, extends, and binds together the varied uses of the term *via*.

will not—they cannot—be fully perfected until the next life. For now, we remain wayfarers. The final goal of all of our journeying is perfection of the virtues, which is another way of saying that we are finally one with Christ.

§1 The Unity of Analogy, Beatitude, and Virtue

When Thomas treats the virtues, he treats the morality of beatitude.[2] Accordingly when Thomas first introduces the virtues, he explains that he must first consider beatitude: "Here we must consider first the ultimate end of human life and then the things through which a human is able to arrive at that end or deviate from it; for it is on the basis of the end that one must ascertain the character of what is ordered to that end" (ST 1-2.1.Prologue). Beatitude defines the virtues that enable us to attain it. Beatitude defines the character of the virtues.

Because beatitude and virtue form a single aspect of Thomas' vision of our destiny, this chapter takes up Thomas' treatment of both under the conceptual umbrella that they share in the *Summa*—the notion of analogy. Is analogy fundamentally important for interpreting Thomas' work? Reinhard Hütter claims that "there is simply no instance in Thomas's work where analogy is not tacitly presupposed or being treated without being named or simply being silently at work in the exercise of *sacra doctrina* itself."[3] To contemporary moral theologians, Hütter's claim about analogy sounds bold and surprising because the notion of analogy does not seem essential to Thomas' writing on the virtues. Accordingly readers of Thomas' writing on the virtues seldom read literature devoted to Thomas' notion of analogy.[4]

This is a mistake. Analogy is indeed "tacitly presupposed" throughout the *Summa Theologiae*, "being treated without being named" and "silently

---

2. Pinckaers, "Beatitude and the Beatitudes," 117. Pinckaers' *Sources of Christian Ethics* outlines how this "morality of beatitude" was underappreciated by inheritors of Thomas.

3. Hütter, "Attending to the Wisdom of God," 214.

4. On virtue as an analogical term: I have uncovered only a few works—Yearley, *Mencius and Aquinas*; Jordan, *Rewritten Theology*, 158–63; McInerny, "The Analogy of Virtue." On analogy: from early seminal works like McInerny, *The Logic of Analogy*, and Burrell, *Analogy and Philosophical Language* to works of more recent note such as Rocca, *Speaking the Incomprehensible God*; Montagnes, *The Doctrine of the Analogy of Being*; Velde, *Aquinas on God*; and the collected volume *The Analogy of Being*, ed. Thomas Joseph White.

at work," especially in his moral teaching.[5] In this chapter I give evidence of the thoroughness of Thomas' analogical understanding in the *Summa* by turning specifically to the analogical terms "beatitude" and "virtue." The picture that emerges shows analogy to be a thread running throughout the *Summa* that facilitates Thomas' conceptual complexity in regards to our language about God and, in turn, our language about ourselves. Analogy allows us to predicate perfection terms (such as "beatitude" and "virtue") of both God and creatures while avoiding the fallacies of equivocation and univocalism. Instead these perfections are said of God and creatures in neither the exact same sense nor in a wholly different sense. To put the same insight negatively: if God did not exist or if God were a phantom, "beatitude" and "virtue" in the way that Thomas predicates them would totally lose their meaning.

Our origin and end is God, attained through Christ. I follow Thomas in attending to God's perfections in the full, perfect meaning of "beatitude" and "virtue" in Christ. In turning to Christ, I add to these moral considerations the core conviction of his theological anthropology: human as made to the *imago Dei* and Christ alone as the Image. For the term "image" is also analogically predicated. "Image," perhaps more obviously than either "beatitude" or "virtue," bears a markedly trinitarian-christological cast and supports the conviction that Christ animates Thomas' moral theology.

What good may come of this exercise? First among reasons, it illustrates another example of what it would be to read the *Summa* as a seamless whole, drawing upon Thomas' ubiquitous treatment of analogy, beatitude, virtues, and God. Scholars of Thomas now widely acknowledge the need for such readings. In casting a wide net, I am constrained to a superficial treatment of several questions. Nevertheless, I hope the bare outline is suggestive. Second among reasons, it endows the language of "virtue" with a remarkable range. That "virtue" especially is not regarded as an analogical term might explain why so much contemporary moral reflection falls flat. Commonly, interpreters ground virtue from the transcendental realm to envisage Christ as merely human exemplar. What could be more mundane? Last among the reasons I list, this exercise is compelling for what it assumes and what it then argues. It assumes that what we say of God is of first importance. It is only because of our understanding of God that we can properly understand human beatitude and human virtue. Therefore the horizon of Thomas' discourse about God frames discussions of our beatitude

---

5. Hütter, "Attending to the Wisdom of God," 214.

and our virtue. Everything is animated by the premise that God stands as the font of all perfection.

§2 A Primer on Analogy

A small cottage industry has sprung up around Thomas' developments of the notion of analogy. Indeed I must rely on this scholarship to offer some explanation of the contours of Thomas' analogical understanding in the *Summa*. Moreover, *which* interpreter I choose makes all the difference for how this notion plays itself out in Thomas' writing. While Ralph McInerny nicely underscores the "the logic of analogy" in Thomas, and Bernard Montagnes brings out its *onto*-logical depth, Rudi te Velde navigates Thomas' middle way.[6] Te Velde retrieves "what seems to be a less theory-loaded, more contextual and intuitive way in which Thomas himself employs the notion of analogy" while concluding that it remains "firmly rooted in the metaphysical conception of being as the intelligible aspect under which the world of creatures is positively related to its divine origin."[7] To state the same approach inversely, te Velde identifies in Thomas a metaphysical basis for analogy without suffocating it with metaphysical theory.[8]

Te Velde begins with Thomas' systematic inquiry about God to develop the terms of the problem that analogy is supposed to solve in Question 13, Article 5 of the *Prima Pars* (ST 1.13.5). Accordingly te Velde follows Thomas step by step as he investigates human discourse on God with the ontological investigation of the mode of God's being (qq3–11), the epistemological investigation of how God can be known (q12), and finally how *human* names can be names of *God* (q13). This investigative, intuitive

---

6. Rocca is also attentive to this middle way, even displaying how McInerny's and Montagnes' seemingly opposed positions on whether "analogy" is logical or ontological (albeit shared in opposition to Cajetan) can in fact be harmonized ("Analogy as Judgment and Faith," 39). More recently, authors including Cessario and Hochschild have drawn attention to the plausibility of Cajetan's interpretation in "Cardinal Cajetan and His Critics," 109–18, and *The Semantics of Analogy*, respectively.

7. Velde, *Aquinas on God*, 97. Te Velde explains the significance of his contextual retrieval of analogy: "The theory of analogy—especially the so-called *analogia entis* as the formula of the metaphysical continuity-in-difference between the world and God—is largely a product of the Thomistic school" and it has obscured Thomas' own notion "by its baroque and proliferated interpretations of analogy" (ibid.).

8. Ibid., 109.

approach to analogy in the *Summa* is crucial because, as te Velde explains, it is the form of inquiry employed by Thomas himself.[9]

It is with a guarded sense of irony, then, that from te Velde's (and Thomas') more discursive approach I plan to extract and condense some of te Velde's conclusions regarding Thomas' use of analogy. Moreover, isolating the key features of analogy in the *Prima Pars* in this section allows me to trace it through the *Secunda Pars* in subsequent sections. To begin summarizing te Velde's interpretation of Thomas: the metaphysical background giving rise to the meaning of analogy is comprised by two integrally related aspects that condition each other: (1) the analogy of being, implying that there is a relation between the two things named in such a way that *one is named from the other* and designates something *belonging to a different genus* (i.e., "transgeneric"), and (2) analogical causality of creation, which as cause-effect captures a certain imperfect "likeness" in creatures based on their diminished and partial "*participation*" of the "form" of the cause.[10] These two aspects apply to names common to creatures and God with analogous language capturing the difference from and likeness to the Creator that creatures enjoy. Te Velde writes,

> From the way in which it is introduced in Question 13 one gets the impression that [analogy] presents itself as a plausible alternative to the two unacceptable extremes of pure equivocity and simple univocity. We speak of analogy when a name is said of two things, neither in exactly the same sense nor in a wholly different sense, but according to a certain relationship of one to another. Thomas does not elaborate on the precise nature of that relationship. It seems to be enough to point out that the perfections of creatures pre-exist in God in a more excellent way. God is, thus, not wholly different from creatures, or better: creatures are not wholly different from God, since they are from God. They bear a certain likeness to God. What kind of likeness? It is a likeness, Thomas explains, according to a certain analogy . . . It is this idea of a remote and diminished likeness of the effect that Thomas tries to articulate in terms of analogy.[11]

Whereas te Velde follows the *ordus disciplinae* to bring out the metaphysical underpinnings of analogy, Gregory Rocca backs into the metaphysics through an intertextual reading that takes up different semantic

---

9. Ibid., 96–97.
10. Ibid., 111–13; see Montagnes, *Doctrine of the Analogy of Being*, 34–43.
11. Velde, *Aquinas on God*, 112–13.

pieces of Thomas' treatment. Rocca turns to Thomas' linguistic clues such as *per prius et posterius* to generate an in-depth treatment of Thomas' notion of analogy. Throughout Thomas' career, Rocca writes, Thomas "uses the phrase *per prius et posterius* to denote how analogous names signify according to an interwoven web of primary and secondary meanings."[12] *Per prius et posterius* is more literally translated *through the prior and posterior*, but probably best rendered *primarily and secondarily*. Unpacking these terms, Rocca explains, "By *prius* Thomas is referring to what he variously calls the perfect, total, proper, or complete meaning, which is predicated absolutely and primarily, whereas by *posterius* he is referring to the imperfect meaning, which is predicated relatively and secondarily."[13] By Rocca's reading, the common analogical term is predicated of one thing according to its perfect and absolute meaning and of other things only imperfectly and relatively; it is predicated of one thing according to its total and complete meaning and of other things only partially and incompletely.[14] All of the varied meanings of an analogical name properly belong to one first meaning—the perfect, absolute, total, and complete meaning—referring to "one" individual reality or nature.[15] Therefore the primary signification of an analogical term such as "being" or "good" is not its meaning or conceptualization, but *God*.

In fact, Thomas demonstrates an initial wariness to apply the flexible phrase *per prius et posterius* to something as fixed as the rapport between God and creation, according to Rocca's reading of Thomas' corpus.[16] *Per prius et posterius* appears too pliant to fit with the relation of cause-effect, which requires the relation of one-to-one. (In contrast, predicamental analogy is open to different relations, e.g., one-to-one; many-to-one;

---

12. Rocca, *Speaking the Incomprehensible God*, 135.

13. Ibid., 137. Rocca draws from *Sententia super Metaphysicam* 7.4, *Scriptum super libros Sententiarum* 2.42, *Quaestiones disputatae de veritate* 1.2, and ST 1.16 and 1.33.

14. Rocca, *Speaking the Incomprehensible God*, 137. Rocca goes on to clarify why this is *not* univocal but analogical. See the following footnote.

15. Not something "one" in essence or meaning; not "one" as in specification or conceptualization, but "one" reality or nature. In speaking this way, Rocca argues, Thomas protects the peculiar logical status of analogy from "the depredations of conceptualist or univocist misinterpretations" (*Speaking the Incomprehensible God*, 141). Rocca treats rival construals of analogy in *Speaking the Incomprehensible God*, chapter 7, and in "Analogy as Judgment and Faith," chapter 10.

16. Rocca, *Speaking the Incomprehensible God*, 141–43. I rely on Rocca's treatment in the paragraph that follows. For more on the priority of one type of analogy, one-to-one, see Wippel, *Metaphysical Thought of Thomas Aquinas*, 82–84 and 568–70.

A Roadmap

two-to-a-third.) Rocca follows Thomas' judgment from an initial rejection of the phrase *per prius et posterius* to describe God and creatures in Thomas' commentary on the *Sentences*, next to Thomas' varied use in *Summa Contra Gentiles* and *Quaestiones Disputate de Potentia Dei*, and finally to Thomas' solution in the *Summa*. Once Thomas constrains the use of analogical causality of creation to a direct relation of one-to-one, he allows that transcendentals can be predicated *per prius* of God. It is worth noting two elements in the genesis of Thomas' judgments: (1) his driving concern to uphold God's transcendence as he discriminates among different types of analogy and (2) the eventual priority of one type of analogy: one-to-one. These elements inform what I take to be an interconnected web of primary and secondary meanings of moral terms in Thomas' moral teaching resulting from an analogical knowledge of God's relations to creatures and creatures' relations to God.

To conclude this primer on analogy, I turn to the analogical terms "beatitude" and "virtue." Thomas begins the *Secunda Pars*, "Now that we have talked about the exemplar, viz., God . . . it remains for us to consider his image, i.e., the human."[17] Thomas turns to the perfection of the image of God in us, a perfection that is similar to—but ultimately more different from—the perfection of God.[18] As Thomas treats the perfection open to us humans, he tells us that God is the Omega, the *Finis* of all.[19] God is the "ultimate end of the human and of all other things."[20] All other ends are defined in relation to this end and such ends in fact preexist as a whole in God's simple perfection. Similarly, in the *Prima Pars* Thomas holds that "a rational creature's ultimate end, *qua* thing, is God."[21] God is Beatitude. "God's beatitude includes every beatitude" such that "whatever is desirable in any sort of beatitude—whether true beatitude or false beatitude—preexists as a whole more eminently in God's beatitude."[22] So too with virtues. "Virtue" is said of God and creatures because of the ordering of creatures to God by God and because of the participation in God by creatures. These

---

17. ST 1.2.Prologue.

18. Fourth Lateran Council: "Between the Creator and the creature so great a likeness cannot be noted without the necessity of noting a greater dissimilarity between them." Cited in Denzinger, *Sources of Catholic Dogma*, no. 432 (171).

19. Thomas derives scriptural support from Rev 1:8, 21:6, and 22:13.

20. ST 1-2.1.8.

21. ST 1.26.3.ad 2. Special thanks to Sean Larsen for drawing my attention to this question.

22. ST 1.26.4.sc. et co.

perfections exist, to the extent that they exist in creatures through God's causality, in a more excellent way in God.[23]

Thomas' analogical understanding of "beatitude" and "virtue" is seldom appreciated for its full metaphysical depth, but sounding these depths discloses their human possibility and their actuality in God—the Ultimate End of Beatitude and Virtue Itself. Moreover, as rooted in the *Secunda Pars* these terms not only echo the Divine Nature of the *Prima Pars* but also point forward to the *Tertia Pars* where we see beatitude and virtue in the flesh: Jesus Christ.

§3 Beatitude: Aristotelian Beginning, Supernatural End

Thomas begins both the *Prima Pars* and the *Secunda Pars* on the note of beatitude. Whereas Thomas writes much of the *Prima Pars* from the perspective of God, he writes the *Secunda Pars* from the level of human action. Thomas makes this difference of perspective especially clear in the *Prologue* of the *Secunda Pars* where he articulates the shift from exemplar to image. This shift emphasizes a critical hermeneutic: that we readers understand the image derives from the exemplar. Thus it forms a "hinge" between the *Prima Pars* and *Secunda* Pars, such that "it shows God laying a foundation, free will, which will support all that follows: morality viewed as the human's return to God," writes Pinckaers, "Nor should we forget that finally, in the *Tertia Pars*, St. Thomas will study Christ who, in his humanity, is the necessary way to God, while in his divine personality Christ is the Word of God, the perfect Image of the Father."[24] An analogical understanding frames the entirety of Thomas' theological synthesis in the *Summa*.

Thus Thomas begins not only where the Lord Himself (in the Sermon on the Mount) and Augustine begin, but where Aristotle begins: humans naturally desire beatitude. In one of Thomas' first opportunities to cite an authority in the *Secunda Pars*, he cites Aristotle to claim that all human acts are for the sake of an end.[25] Thomas affirms Aristotle throughout the

---

23. ST 1.13.6. Jordan (*Rewritten Theology*, 160) argues that the definition of virtue to which all others are analogous is in ST 1-2.55.4, whereas I locate it in Thomas' language regarding God.

24. Pinckaers, "Ethics and the Image of God," 132–33.

25. That is, the *sed contra* of the first article of the first question (ST 1-2.1.1.sc.). In Thomas' questions on beatitude, Thomas cites Scripture sixty times, the commentaries

first four articles of this question's eight articles: nature too acts for an end (1.2.sc.), the good entails positing an ultimate end (1.4.sc.), and there are not infinite causes because of the existence of a first mover (1.4.co. et ad2). These first four articles assert, as Aristotle asserts, that there is a final aim to activity. Thus Aristotle and Thomas share a sense of a natural finality. Pinckaers puts it well: "At the center [of the path to beatitude] there runs the line of finality. Like a spinal column it controls the structure of morality. Thanks to a person's reason, it is proper to her to act in view of an end, which specifies the quality of her acts, and joins them to an ultimate finality which orders her whole life, as well as all her acts."[26]

The ultimate finality which orders each and everything is God, according to Thomas. By introducing the doctrine of God to the discussion, the fifth article also initiates a shift in authorities. Instead of Aristotle, Thomas uses the *sed contras* to cite St. Paul, the Gospel of Matthew, and Augustine. It may seem that Thomas is inclined to abandon Aristotle in his turn to theology, but Thomas actually turns to Aristotle once again in the final article to iterate Aristotle's invocation of a twofold end.[27] Thomas writes,

> As the Philosopher says in *Physics* 2 and *Metaphysics* 5, there are two senses of "end" (*finis*), viz., (a) *finis cuius* and (b) *finis quo*—i.e., (a) *the thing itself* (*ipsa res*) in which the concept of the good is found and (b) *attaining* (*adeptio*) or *possessing* (*usus*) that thing . . . Therefore, if we are talking about humanity's ultimate end as regards *the thing itself* which is the end, then in this sense all other things share in the human ultimate end, since God is the ultimate end of the human and of all other things. By contrast, if we are talking about humanity's ultimate end as regards *attaining* the end . . . the human and other rational creatures attain the ultimate end by knowing and loving God.[28]

---

of the church fathers sixty-one, and Aristotle sixty-six (Pinckaers, "Beatitude and the Beatitudes," 115). "Because of St. Thomas's discretion," Pinckaers adds, "people were not sufficiently aware of the spiritual and evangelical dimension of the treatise on beatitude, which nonetheless was clearly indicated by numerous quotations from Sts. John, Paul, Matthew, the prophets and the Psalms, as well as from St. Augustine, Pseudo-Dionysius, etc. . . . in the *sed contras* that ordinarily provide the sources for his arguments" ("Aquinas's Pursuit of Beatitude," 103).

26. Pinckaers, "Beatitude and the Beatitudes," 119.

27. ST 1-2.1.8 is an explicit use of Aristotle, whereas implicit ones run through intermediate articles, e.g., ST 1-2.1.7.

28. ST 1-2.1.8.sc.; see too ST 1.26.3.ad2.

Aristotle's understanding of end aids Thomas' argument that there is a single end of human life: God. The doctrine of God grounds the discussion of the two meanings of "end." "End" is said analogously because it applies differently depending on whether we speak of the Ultimate End (God) or the act of attaining it (knowing and loving God). "End" is signified by the first meaning as the thing itself to establish its primary meaning—the perfect, absolute, total, and complete meaning (God). The second meaning of "end" (knowing and loving God) is secondary. It is derivative, deriving its end-ness from the Ultimate End.

The two meanings of "end" appear again in Question 3. The first meaning is "man's ultimate end is an *uncreated* good, namely, God;" the second is "man's ultimate end is something *created* which exists within him and which is nothing other than possessing or enjoying the ultimate end."[29] Therefore Question 3 elaborates the created character of "end" in creatures, making the previous analogical distinction in Question 1 more specific by invoking creation. Thomas' doctrine of creation in the *Prima Pars* entails a likeness of creation to God, the creature to Creator, effect to cause—for a creature "is said to be similar to God not because they share in a form according to the same nature of genus or species, but only because of an analogy, *viz.*, insofar as God is a being through his essence and the others are beings through participation."[30] Question 3, drawing on creation, pertains most clearly to the analogical causality of creation. Pulling Questions 1 and 3 together nicely brings out the simultaneity of the order of being and the analogical causality of creation by claiming that the human's ultimate "end" just is the Ultimate End and it is created by Uncreated Good.

Thomas moves seamlessly from "end" to "beatitude." Whereas "God is beatitude through his essence, since He is blessed through his own essence and not by attaining, or participating in, something else," by contrast, "men are blessed through participation, just as they are said to be 'gods' through participation."[31] The two aspects of analogy stand out clearly—of being and of causation—as each dependent upon the other. Were there no first and universal principle of being—*esse ipsum subsistens*—there would be no *esse* for creatures to participate in thus no "being" to be blessed; were there no Beatitude, there would be no way of predicating beatitude

---

29. ST 1-2.3.1.

30. ST 1.4.3.ad3. The *respondeo* runs: *secundum aliqualem analogiam*, according to a sort of analogy.

31. Quoting Boethius in ST 1-2.3.1.ad1.

of creatures. Beatitude Itself makes possible humanity's beatitude by way of participation; God is the perfect, absolute, total, and complete meaning of "beatitude" and humanity's beatitude is its imperfect, relative, partial, and incomplete meaning. God is the one reality to which all "beatitude" is referred. The manner in which humans possess "beatitude"—real albeit qualified—is brought out by the notion of analogy.[32]

Thomas analogically extends the range of "beatitude" in Question 5 as he discusses how beatitude can be attained.[33] This question elaborates Aristotle's second of two senses, *finis quo*. Indeed, Thomas recalls his earlier treatment explicitly.[34] Thomas writes, "a sort of participation in beatitude can be had in this life, but perfect and genuine beatitude cannot be had in this life."[35] With respect to our act of attaining beatitude, Thomas distinguishes between "perfect and genuine beatitude," which I designate shorthand as perfect, and "a sort of participation in beatitude," which I call imperfect (as later in article 5 of this question Thomas calls it *beatitudo imperfecta*). Perfect beatitude excludes every evil and fulfills every good. It is realized in seeing God's Essence. Such beatitude is the fullest participation in God's life open to us. It is reserved for the future life. Relative to the beatitude open to us in the next life, all beatitude in this life is imperfect. Imperfect beatitude in this life is marked by unfulfilled desire. It is "not yet perfectly happy."[36] As long as we remain wayfarers, "so long as something remains for [us] to desire and seek," we do not yet attain our perfect beatitude.[37]

Thus "perfect" and "imperfect" are relative terms of degree, limited by our creaturely capacities yet fixed by their absolutely perfect referent. Just as our beatitude is imperfect as compares to God's, our beatitude had in this life is imperfect in relationship to our beatitude in seeing God's essence. The first application of perfect and imperfect in Questions 1 and 3 distinguishes between the primary meaning of "beatitude" and its secondary meaning. The second application in Question 5 distinguishes among beatitude's secondary meanings. The qualifiers of perfect and imperfect

---

32. See ST 1-2.62.1.ad1.

33. Thomas anticipates Question 5's extension in Question 3, Article 8 where he contrasts final and perfect beatitude with a "not yet" qualifier. See too *Super Boetium De Trinitate*, 6.4.ad 3.

34. ST 1-2.5.2.

35. ST 1-2.5.3.

36. ST 1-2.3.8.

37. Ibid.

specify the extent to which and in what ways we participate in Beatitude by analogically extending "beatitude." The crucial moment of identity among the various meanings of "beatitude" is *not a meaning at all* but an individual reality—God—to which all the different meanings of "beatitude" necessarily refer.[38]

Chart 1: *Summa Theologiae* 1-2, Questions 1–3

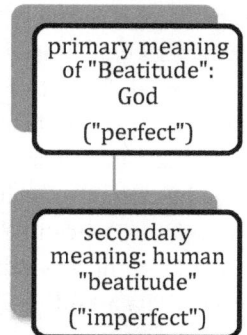

Finally, Question 5 ends as the others do, "break[ing] out of the gates of the City of Reason, not in a desperate sortie, but at full strength and equipment, a theology with all of its philosophy intact."[39] For Thomas assimilates Aristotle's ends to relativize them within an extended analogical range in relation to the Ultimate End. Yet this assimilation entails radical transformation of the then-current meanings.

An even more complex account of humans' end in beatitude is to come. It is prefigured in the *Prima Pars*, where Thomas treats the notion that eventually sets the context for his moral theology: *imago Dei*, destined for beatitude. Thus we must keep the *Prima Pars* in view as we move through the *Secunda Pars*.[40] In the *Prima Pars*, Question 93, Thomas asks whether the image of God is found in every human. The answer is "yes," with three ways in which we see the *imago Dei*: (1) in a natural aptitude for

---

38. Rocca, *Speaking the Incomprehensible God*, 151. As a result, Thomas adds a new analogous sense to the word *ratio*, creating a new analogous meaning for meaning. For a comparable analysis, see McInerny, "Discussion: Analogy Is Analogous," 73–88, and "Analogy Is Analogous," in *Aquinas and Analogy*, 137–41. For McInerny this claim is a crucial interpretive issue in his criticism of Cajetan's presentation of analogous names because it denies that the division of analogous names are of a genus into its species.

39. Gilby, introduction to vol. 16 of Aquinas, *Summa Theologiae*, xiv.

40. Johnson, "An Accomplishment of the Moral Part of Aquinas's *Summa theologiae*," 85–104, esp. 91–94.

understanding and loving God common to all, (2) in habitually knowing and loving God in conformity with grace, and (3) in knowing and loving God perfectly in the likeness of glory. This threefold way in the *Prima Pars* provides the full rationale for establishing the meaning of beatitude in the *Secunda Pars*. This rationale is only partially realized by the time Thomas concludes the *Prima Secundae,* Question 5. Thomas must analogically extend the meaning of "beatitude" even further. He does this in the questions on virtue.

§4 Virtues' Various Ends

Thomas' treatment of the primary meaning of "virtue" finds its completion in the *Tertia Pars*. Nonetheless, there are moments in the *Prima Secundae* where the analogical character of "virtue" stands out with special clarity. One such moment is Question 61, midway through the questions on virtue, when Thomas affirms a traditional division of virtue into four kinds.[41] The exemplar of human virtue, Thomas writes, "must pre-exist in Him, just as the conceptions of all things pre-exist in Him. So, then, virtue can be thought of insofar as it exists in an exemplary way in God (*prout est exemplartier in Deo*), and in this sense [the virtues in question] are called *exemplary virtues*."[42] "Virtue" is predicated *per prius* of God. The perfect, absolute, total, and complete meaning of "virtue" refers to God. Second, "these virtues, are called *political virtues* insofar as by these virtues a human behaves uprightly in conducting human affairs."[43] Thomas goes on to call the political virtues "human." Third and fourth are perfecting and perfect virtues, as "virtues that fall between the political virtues, which are *human* virtues, and the exemplary virtues, which are *divine* virtues. These virtues are distinguished by a diversity of movements and endpoints."[44] Perfecting virtues are of humans on their way and tending towards divine likeness; perfect virtues are of humans who have already attained to divine likeness. With the perfecting and perfect virtues comes a veritable range—political, perfecting, perfect, exemplar—with the meaning of "virtue" found in exemplar virtues.

41. See Mattison's treatment of Thomas' attempt to synthesize traditions in *ST* 1-2.61.5 in "Thomas' Categorizations of Virtue," 189–235.
42. *ST* 1-2.61.5.
43 Ibid.
44 Ibid.

Astute readers are now ready for these virtues to map onto "beatitude," an expectation that is soon fulfilled. In Question 62 Thomas invokes our twofold beatitude, but couples it with the introduction of something new—the theological virtues:

> As is clear from what was said above (1-2.5.7), a human is perfected through acts by which he/she is ordered toward beatitude. But as was explained above (1-2.5.5), humanity's beatitude or happiness is twofold. One sort of beatitude is proportioned to human nature, viz., the beatitude which a human is able to attain through the principles of his/her own nature. The other sort is a beatitude which exceeds humanity's nature and which a human can attain only by God's power, by a certain participation in the divine nature (*secundum quandam divinitatis participationem*)—this according to 2 Peter 1:4, which says that through Christ we are made "partakers of the divine nature." Since this second sort of beatitude exceeds a proportion to human nature, a human's natural principles, by which he/she proceeds to act well in a way proportioned to his nature (*secundum suam proportionem*), are not sufficient for ordering the human toward this beatitude. Hence, principles by which he/she might be so ordered toward supernatural beatitude have to be divinely added to a human—in just the way in which he/she is ordered by his/her natural principles toward his/her connatural end (though not without God's help). And these principles are called *theological virtues*, not only because (a) they have God as their object, but also because (b) they are infused in us by God alone and because (c) these virtues are made known (*traduntur*) to us only through divine revelation, in Sacred Scripture.[45]

This crucial article marks our arrival at what Pinckaers calls, after beatitude and before evangelical law, the "second towering peak" of the *Secunda Pars*. It is shot through with Thomistic analogy. It alludes to the questions on beatitude to describe a twofold beatitude, "one is proportioned to human nature" and the other "a certain participation in the divine nature." The theological virtues are not essentially human but ours by participation. They are proportionate to us in accord with our *participated nature*.[46] Moreover the theological virtues are "exemplate" virtues named from the divine exemplar virtues because by them we are made virtuous by God and

---

45. ST 1-2.62.1.

46. ST 1-2.62.1.ad1. Cf. Williams' claim that Thomas' reply to the first objection "is the first of the analogical relationships Thomas proposes in Question 62" (*Ground of Union*, 36).

A Roadmap

in relation to God.[47] Theological virtues are necessary to direct our reason and will toward God, for

> reason and will are ordered toward God naturally in the sense that God is the principle and end of human nature, yet in a way proportioned to the nature. But human reason and will are not by their nature adequately ordered toward God insofar as He is the object of supernatural beatitude.[48]

Even our powers of "reason" and "will" are analogical terms whose primary meanings derive from Thomas' doctrine of God.[49]

The analogical terms "beatitude" and "virtue" condition one another to such an extent that "the *Secunda Pars* may accurately be described as the morality of beatitude."[50] William Mattison notes that the new question of "natural versus supernatural virtues reminds the reader of Thomas' discussion of the different types of [beatitude] (see ST 1-2.3.8 and 5.5), but discussion of the impact of the two types of [beatitude] on virtue is not fully clear until 1-2.61.1."[51] Mattison's observations move from beatitude to virtues. This seems right. But I also pose the complementary question: how does Thomas' introduction of the theological virtues impact Thomas' prior discussion of beatitude?

Arguably Thomas' new treatment of virtues complexifies his existing account of beatitude.[52] Recall the range of "beatitude" covered by the first

---

47. ST 1-2.62.1.ad2: *non sunt exemplares sed exemplatae*.

48. ST 1-2.62.1.ad3.

49. A. N. Williams puts it well: "The dynamic relation of intellect and will determines the structure of both his doctrine of the Trinity and his theological anthropology. If we follow the development of Thomas' argument, we see that while the root principle of the *Prima Pars* is simplicity, simplicity's correlates are intellect and will, and the culmination of the *De Deo uno* forms the foundation of the *De Trinitate* and the anthropology. It is precisely this link, the analogy between the structure of the divine nature and the divine person, that provides the basis for the Thomist doctrine of deification" (*Ground of Union*, 36).

50. Pinckaers, "Beatitude and the Beatitudes," 117, a "morality of beatitude" that was underappreciated by Thomas' inheritors.

51. Mattison, "Thomas' Categorizations of Virtue," 218 n. 89.

52. De Lubac treats the same questions, viz., ST 1-2.5 and 62 in "*Duplex Hominis Beatitudo*," 290–99. De Lubac denies the Thomistic doctrine of "two orders" and "pure nature." His conclusions are generated from his interpretive fuzziness. Puzzling over controversial Question 62, de Lubac uses Question 5 to reify Question 62. That is, he reads Question 62 as merely iterating the distinction from Question 5. (Indeed, the cross-referencing in many English translations could lead others to support this mistaken

five questions of the *Prima Secundae*. Beatitude is predicated *per prius* of God *et posterius* of humans (Questions 1 and 3). Moreover "beatitude" enjoys a range of predications for humans: *perfect beatitude* consists in our seeing God's essence whereas ours is *imperfect beatitude* in this life (Question 5). As perfect and imperfect are relative terms that Thomas applies and reapplies, Question 5 does not identify a fixed evaluation of "beatitude" but rather brings out the difference between "beatitude" as it is predicated of our eschatological life in God and "beatitude" as it is predicated of this life. Question 62 on the theological virtues extends the range of analogical predications of "beatitude" even further. It builds on Question 5's "beatitude" in this life—*imperfect beatitude*—to suggest that "beatitude" in this life may refer to *supernatural beatitude* or *natural beatitude*. *Supernatural beatitude* is obtained by a kind of participation in the Godhead through the theological virtues whereas *natural beatitude*, proportionate to human nature, is obtained by means of our natural principles.

Chart 2: *Summa Theologiae* 1-2, Question 5

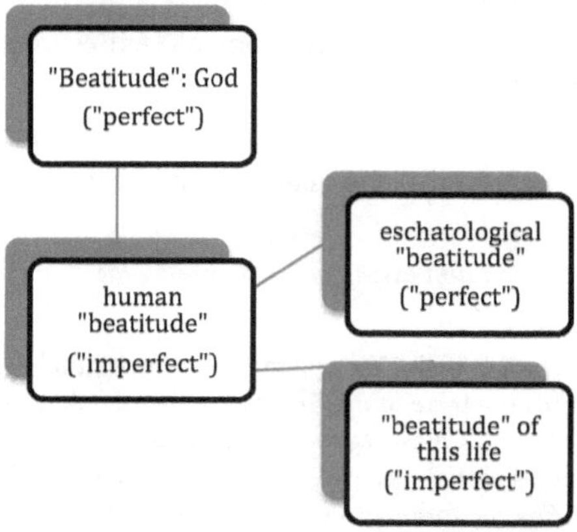

```
"Beatitude": God
   ("perfect")
       |
       |                    eschatological
       |                       "beatitude"
       |                       ("perfect")
   human                  /
   "beatitude"  ---------
   ("imperfect")          \
                           "beatitude" of
                              this life
                            ("imperfect")
```

The terms perfect and imperfect may be helpful, but we use them carefully. We might call *supernatural beatitude* perfect and *natural beatitude* imperfect, but both *supernatural* and *natural beatitude* are located in the context of this life, which is itself *imperfect beatitude* relative to *perfect* eschatological *beatitude*. Moreover even our *perfect* eschatological *beatitude* is imperfect relative to the singular and unqualifiedly perfect, complete, absolute, and total meaning of beatitude.

---

conclusion.) Thus he denies Question 62's twofold beatitude—as defined by a natural and supernatural end—in this life.

A Roadmap

Returning to Question 62, relative to one another the virtues directed toward our *supernatural beatitude* are perfect and *natural beatitude*, imperfect. Question 62's invocation of "virtue" to analogically extend "beatitude" is just the elaboration needed for beatitude to map on to the prior treatment ST 1.94 invoked at the end of the previous section where Thomas names the three ways in which we see the *imago Dei*: (1) in a natural aptitude, (2) in a supernatural aptitude of grace, and (3) in the likeness of glory. Natural aptitude concerns our perfection in *natural beatitude*. Supernatural aptitude concerns our perfection in *supernatural beatitude*. And the likeness of glory concerns our eschatological destiny. The rest of Thomas' analysis of the virtues in the *Secunda Pars* largely brackets our eschatological perfection in favor of elaborating the imperfect beatitude available in this life, in which one is perfect (*supernatural*) relative to the other (*natural*).[53] Thomas drops these brackets, so to speak, in the *Tertia Pars* when "virtue" in Christ surpasses all human analogates.

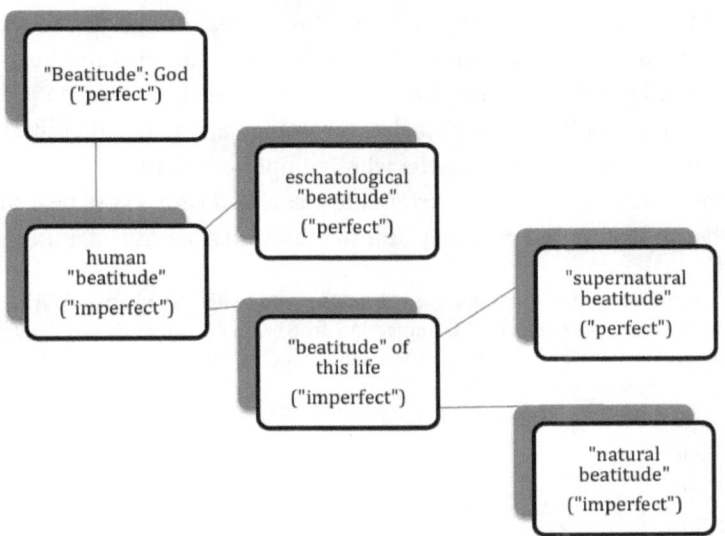

Chart 3: Summa Theologiae 1-2, Question 62

Still in the context of *imperfect beatitude,* though in a slightly different vein, Thomas develops his analogical understanding of virtues and

---

53. Contrary to appearances, Thomas does not end his treatment of the virtues with just two kinds: (1) theological virtue concerning supernatural beatitude and (2) cardinal virtues concerning natural beatitude. Thomas has yet to introduce (3) *infused moral virtues*, whose hybridity resists (too) simple mapping that has to do with theological and cardinal (ST 1-2.63).

beatitude in Question 65 of the *Summa*. Article 2 of the *Quaestio Disputata de Virtutibus Cardinalibus* unfolds similarly.[54] Article 2 is especially helpful since it distinguishes virtues based on the end toward which they are directed. To wit, in Article 2 virtues are distinguished by being (1) unqualifiedly perfect, (2) perfect in one way, and (3) wholly imperfect. First, unqualifiedly perfect virtues are combined with charity. They "make a human action unqualifiedly good, in that it is something that attains our ultimate end."[55] Second, virtues perfect-in-one-way consist in virtues which achieve right reason, "but do not reach God himself through charity."[56] They are perfect in relation to the human good, "but do not attain the first standard, which is our ultimate end."[57] As such, these virtues are "perfect-in-one-way," not unqualifiedly.[58] Third, wholly imperfect virtues are inclinations that do not possess the character of a virtue because, among other reasons, they are open to misuse. Although they do not possess the character of a virtue in a perfect way, they are still "virtue." (That they are so underscores the incredible range of the analogical term "virtue.") Again, this threefold distinction is helpful in its ability to pick out virtue's realization of its end. The cases for the first two are obvious: virtues perfect-in-one-way are perfect in relation to natural beatitude, but imperfect in relation to supernatural beatitude. Unqualifiedly perfect virtues are perfect in relation to the ultimate end of supernatural beatitude. (Nonetheless, even they are qualified eschatologically.) But what of the third—the wholly imperfect virtues? Thomas gives evidence elsewhere that false virtues are associated with a false beatitude—false because of the likeness they bear to their *vera et perfecta* counterpart.[59]

---

54. Aquinas, *Quaestio disputata de virtutibus cardinalibus* (hereafter QDVC), 2, in *Disputed Questions on Virtue*. In connection to ST 1-2.65, these disputed questions are thought to have been written at the same time as Thomas was working on the corresponding parts of the *Summa*, 1268–72 AD.

55. QDVC, 2.

56. Ibid.

57. Ibid.

58. Ibid.

59. See "*falsa est virtus*" in ST 1-2.65.2. Etienne Gilson glosses this passage: "An extreme expression, which departs from St. Thomas's usual terminology. He prefers, as we have seen, to say that these are virtues, albeit imperfect virtues. That they are false in the order of supernatural merit, and this is what St. Augustine means, St. Thomas readily admits. When St. Thomas speaks of them as relatively true, or true in a certain sense, or under a certain relationship (*secundum quid*), he is maintaining, on a plane which does not interest St. Augustine, that they deserve the name of virtue in the exact measure in which they satisfy the definition of virtue. To the extent that each of them realizes this, it is a virtue."

A Roadmap

Throughout his treatment of the virtues, Thomas returns to an important point: even perfect-in-one-way virtues, as actions proportionate to human nature, are "not without God's help."[60] They are "not without God."[61] Humans "need God's help in order to be moved by Him toward acting well."[62] Thomas lends a surprising theological gloss even to virtues whose end is natural beatitude. (This transformation entails a further recognition of the effects of sin on our ability to attain even natural beatitude.[63]) What is more, we learn from Thomas that even unqualifiedly perfect virtues, which are directed to our supernatural beatitude, require cultivation and habituation as they lack the *delectatio* characteristic of virtues directed toward natural beatitude.[64] This lack likens the two kinds of virtues—perfect-in-one-way and unqualifiedly perfect—insofar as they both fall short of their eschatological completion. Thomas' use of analogical terms constantly signify and, if we allow them, direct our attention to the ground of our every (imperfect) perfection.

Thomas' treatment of our "virtue" *in this life* remains incomplete, as does his treatment of our "beatitude," until both find their completion in Question 69 of the *Prima Secundae*, "The Beatitudes." This question is strategically placed as the capstone to his treatise on the virtues. It describes the summit and perfection of the Christian life, animated by Christ's own response to the question of beatitude. Moving along this path of beatitude requires that one advance "through the works of the virtues" and be "led toward it by the Holy Spirit," for "it is through the gifts that we are perfected in being obedient to Him and in following Him."[65] This journey reaches its consummation in the beatitudes as perfect acts—perfect virtues completed by the gifts of the Holy Spirit. "Thus, through the virtues and gifts," Pinckaers writes, "the most finished spiritual work is achieved, the fulfillment of the Beatitudes. It is like a fruit which has come to full maturity."[66] Indeed,

---

60. ST 1-2.62.1.

61. Aquinas, *De veritate*, 24.14; also see objection 5 and its reply on "imago."

62. ST 1-2.109.2.

63. Along similar lines Thomas Joseph White qualifies his high praise for Lawrence Feingold's *Natural Desire to See God*: "One aspect in the study that is underemphasized or that could be considered an important addendum is a consideration of the effects of sin upon the attainment of the natural ends of the human person (natural knowledge and natural love of God)." White, review of Feingold, 466.

64. For a development of this striking idea and its implications, see Schockenhoff, *Bonum hominis*, 291–320.

65. ST 1-2.69.1.

66. Pinckaers, "Beatitude and the Beatitudes," 124–25. Pinckaers notes that the happy

Thomas describes our hope for future beatitude as "the hope one has when the first fruits have already begun to appear."[67] In these fruits, the evangelical Beatitudes, we see an "imperfect beginning of future beatitude" starting "even in this life."[68]

§5 A Glimpse of Our Ultimate End in Christ

In the culmination of his treatise on virtues, Thomas claims that the answer to human desire is patterned off of Christ's own response to the question of beatitude. The answer consists in following Christ's example of the virtues. This eschatological, christological conclusion midway through the *Prima Secundae* is the outgrowth of Thomas' claim that we are made to the image of God. In a broader sense, Thomas thematizes this theological insight throughout the *Summa* in the way he organizes its parts: God in the *Prima Pars*, humans as *imago Dei* in the *Secunda Pars*, Christ in the *Tertia Pars*. Therefore it should not come as a surprise—although it has suffered from inattention—that *imago Dei* carries serious christological weight. Thomas' moral theology shows its debts to Christ everywhere, but everywhere subtly.[69]

The rich theology of *imago Dei* has been the subject of much new literature that reaffirms its importance.[70] I complement this work by sketching how Thomas also uses "image" as an analogical term. In barest outline: Thomas cites Colossians 1:15 and Genesis 1:26 to describe Christ as *the Image of the invisible God* and humans as *to/toward Our own image*. Thomas' implied analogical grades in perfection follow the order outlined above. Indeed, for Thomas "image" is another way of talking about "beatitude" and "virtue." But what is newly fecund is Thomas' claims about the One Who serves as *both*—Christ is both Exemplar and human exemplar, perfect Image of the Father and perfect image of God in the human.

---

unity of Beatitudes, virtues, and gifts is extended into the structure of the ST 2-2.

67. ST 1-2.69.2.

68. Ibid.

69. For sustained attention to this thesis, see Wawrykow, "Jesus in the Moral Theology of Thomas Aquinas," 13–33.

70. Magisterial documents include *Gaudium et Spes* and the International Theological Commission's "Communion and Stewardship." Thomists have been especially keen to reaffirm this theology, notes Di Noia, footnoting more than ten recent pieces in "*Imago Dei—Imago Christi,*" 19–30.

A Roadmap

Thomas thinks that in our perfect imaging of God's perfection, we image God analogically. This is another way of saying that even our perfect imaging of God is similar to, but ultimately more different from, the perfection of God. Thomas explains why by invoking Hilary of Poitiers:

> In *De Synodis* Hilary says, "An image is not different in species (*species indifferens*) from the thing it is an image of." And, again, he says, "An image is an undivided and unified likeness of a thing, meant to equate that thing with another thing." But God and a human do not share the same species (*non est species indifferens Dei et hominis*); nor can a human have equality with God.[71]

Rather, Thomas clarifies, we are one with God or like God "in accord with a certain analogy or proportion."[72] Thomas signals this imperfection—that the image is imperfect, relative, partial, and incomplete in us—by saying that the human is *ad imaginem*. Scripture states that the human is *ad imaginem* in Genesis 1:26, *Let Us make humans to Our own image and likeness*, when it says that the human was made "to the image of God (*ad imaginem Dei*). For the preposition 'to' (*ad*) signifies the approach of something that is far off in the distance (*accessum quendam qui competit rei distanti*)."[73] This preposition "ad" meaning "to" is crucial, as Thomas himself highlights, because it denotes a movement toward or approach to God rather than having arrived—always *in via*. In this little word *ad*, "a small bit of grammar carries a good deal of theology."[74]

Who is the image of the invisible God, the First-born of every creature but Christ (Col 1:15)? Christ is the *Image* unqualifiedly, perfectly.[75] More than once Thomas marks the differences in how humans and Christ image God by using the following metaphor:

> There are two ways in which an image of something may be found in a given thing. In one way, it exists in a thing which has the same nature with respect to its species—in the way, for instance, that the image of a king exists in his own son. In the second way, it exists in a thing with a different nature—in the way that the image of the king exists on a coin. It is in the first way that the Son is the Image of the Father, whereas it is in the second way that the human is

---

71. ST 1.93.1.obj 3.
72. ST 1.93.1.ad3.
73. ST 1.93.1.co; 35.2.ad3.
74. Kerr, *After Aquinas*, 124.
75. ST 1.93.1.ad2.

called the image of God ... The human is not only called an image (*imago*) but is said to be "to the image" (*ad imaginem*).[76]

This passage identifies the explanatory principle for the differences between the Son and a human: the Son is one in nature with the Father; a human is of a different nature. The first instance of "image" works univocally, whereas the second works analogically. This is why it is appropriate to apply *Image* to Christ without qualification, whereas, again, it is better said that the human is not the *image* but *to the image*.

The relationship between Father and Son reveals the relationship between Exemplar and Image. Thomas states, "that in whose likeness something proceeds is properly called an exemplar," and clarifies that "an image, properly speaking, proceeds in the likeness of the other."[77] The Son proceeds from the Father in eternal generation in his perfect likeness. Thus, Thomas and Augustine both assert that *the Son alone is the Image of the Father*.[78] *Image* is strictly identified with the second person of the Trinity.

When considering the necessity and fittingness of the Incarnation, Thomas echoes the classic preoccupation of the church fathers—*what is a human that he should follow the King, his maker?* (Eccl 2:12). He infuses his *Commentary on the Letters of Saint Paul to the Corinthians* with analogical principles:

> Now the primordial principle of the production of things is the Son of God: *all things were made through Him* (John 1:3). He is, therefore, the primordial exemplar, which all creatures imitate as the true and perfect Image of the Father. Hence it is said: *He is the Image of the invisible God, the first-born of every creature, for in Him all things were created* (Col 1:15). But in a special way He is the exemplar of spiritual graces, with which spiritual creatures are endowed, as is said to the Son *in the splendors of the saints before the morning star I begot you* (Ps 110:3), namely, because He was begotten before every creature through resplendent grace, having in Himself as exemplar the splendors of all the saints. But this exemplar of God has been very remote from us at first, as it is said: *what is a man that he should follow the King, his maker?* (Eccl 2:12) And therefore He willed to become a human, that He might offer humans a human exemplar.[79]

76. ST 1.35.2; see also, for example, 93.1.
77. ST 1.35.1.ad1.
78. ST 1.35.2.sc.
79. Aquinas, *Commentary on Corinthians*, 1 Cor 11:1, no. 583. I am indebted to

A Roadmap

Incarnation is the Word's answer to how a human might *follow the King, his maker*. The Incarnate Word as *Word* is the "primordial exemplar," the "true and perfect Image of the Father" and "Image of the invisible God" (drawing upon Col 1:15). The Incarnate Word as *Incarnate* is the Word's becoming human to offer humans a "human exemplar." As the Word, Christ is the Image of the Father. As Incarnate, Christ is the perfect image of God in the human.

Christ's unique identity as the Incarnate Word requires a correspondingly unique exercise in analogical thinking. Christ is fully God, the Word—and in this sense we speak of Christ's perfection in Beatitude and Virtue as the Image of God analogically. Christ is fully human, Incarnate—and in this sense we speak of Christ's perfection in beatitude and virtue as the image of God univocally.[80]

The analogical use of "image" is familiar. We have seen this use of "image" time and again in Thomas' trinitarian considerations: the Son shares the divine nature with the Father; the Son alone is the Image of the Father. He alone is Beatitude and Virtue, the "primordial exemplar." But he is also a "human exemplar." The univocal use of "image" is singular. It commands our attention to the mystery of the Incarnation. The Son of God became one of us. The Son of God is one of us. And the Son of God is one with us, with a nature identical to ours. Christ Incarnate is the perfect human, the perfect image of God, perfect in virtue—"the unfailing exemplar of holiness," "exemplar of the splendors of all the saints,"[81] the supreme exemplar of perfection[82]—and perfectly beatified.[83]

Christ is the human exemplar, the true human, whose nature is perfectly and most fully expressed by the Word in the Incarnation. Thomas takes pains to clarify that scriptural depictions of "Jesus as moral agent have to do with the Word, not as the Word (that divine person), or as God, but precisely as incarnate, that is, as truly human," writes Joseph Wawrykow, "and what holds true of other humans holds true of this human. Jesus did and could do what he did because he had grace and the virtues, which

---

Shanley's "Aquinas's Exemplar Ethics," 345–69, for drawing my attention to this passage.

80. See Marshall, "Christ the End of Analogy," 280–313.

81. Aquinas, *Commentary on Corinthians*, 1 Cor 11:1, no. 583.

82. Aquinas, *Commentary on John*, 12:6, no. 1604.

83. ST 3.32.3; 9.2. White defends this traditional claim from recent objections in "The Voluntary Action of the Earthly Christ," 497–534.

perfected the Word in the Word's taken-up humanity."[84] The Word shows what is possible for those who know and love God.

Gaudium et Spes states, "In reality, it is only in the mystery of the Incarnate Word that the mystery of man truly becomes clear."[85] The Incarnate Word fully reveals to us what it is to be human. He restores the divine image disfigured by sin. He reveals to us our calling to divine beatitude and divine love. He beckons us to imitate Him in perfect virtue. He makes us partakers in the divine nature through Him. In Christ's human actions univocally predicated, He reveals the Word of God to us analogically understood.

In other words, "beatitude," "virtue," and "image" find their full, true, absolutely perfect meaning in Christ. For us, these analogical predications do more than simply mark the limits of our human understanding and achievements. They denote for us the two things above all that must be believed: the mystery of the Trinity and the mystery of the Incarnation[86]

---

84. Wawrykow, "Jesus in the Moral Theology of Thomas Aquinas," 21. Wawrykow notes that Thomas is innovative among the Scholastics for re-narrating the story of Jesus as a human life worth emulating within a *summa*—a systematic statement and reflection on the truths of faith (ibid., 18).

85. Vatican Council II, *Gaudium et Spes*, no. 22.

86. Aquinas, *Commentary on John*, 6:70, no. 1004: "In our faith there are two things above all that must be believed: the mystery of the Trinity, and the Incarnation."

2

Will's Wanderings

Now we meet the wanderer Will and follow him as he wanders through Prologue–Passus IV of *Piers Plowman*. Will is Thomas' human who "naturally desires beatitude" (ST 1.2.1.ad1). For Langland, "Will" is a proper name for the narrator and a personification of a power of the soul—and ostensibly the first name of the author himself.[1]

The immediate impression readers will gather is that Langland treats virtues on a new register. The virtues are not abstracted theological concepts that float above the contingencies of human existence—standing apart from the influence of others, separated from the practices and communities that cultivate and sustain the virtues, ignoring individual and collective questions about agency, shirking the limits of epistemic ambiguity. Instead the virtues are bound up in the material conditions for their flourishing. They are situated in a full-bodied, experiential context. Will's search for salvation and true virtue takes place in *this* setting.

The beginning of *Piers Plowman* positions readers at the nadir of the poem's treatment of virtue. The virtues we find are hollow and false. They are best identified with the allegorized figure of Meed whose errant, implacable desire is to enable the exchange and accumulation of worldly treasure. She takes her cue from the market economy and in turn disorders the socio-political order. Her devastation is so far-reaching that it leaves even those who intend good not knowing how to escape her influence.

---

1. Kane, *Piers Plowman: The Evidence for Authorship*. Cf. Benson, "The Langland Myth."

Considering Meed's mastery of the entire institutional and social worlds, cultivating genuine virtue appears a chimera.

In sum, this episode communicates the complexity of the formation of virtue. It shows how our own desires hardly escape the influence of others, and therefore are never socially or politically neutral. It reminds us that no virtue exists without formation from the practices and communities of which we are a part. It reminds us of the tenacity of epistemic ambiguity, even for honest seekers.

Chapter 2 complements the work of Thomas in chapter 1 by filling out the reality of what Thomas calls "false" virtues associated with false beatitude. Recall that Thomas considers these "false," but virtues all the same because they bear some likeness to their true and perfect counterpart.[2] So too Will finds himself in Meed's world as a result of his initial search for treasure. So too Meed herself shares the same aim. The corruption, manipulation, and threats of violence in this episode help us wayfarers better regard that "treasure" for what it is—false.

The structure of this chapter is twofold, focusing on Meed (Passus II–IV in §1) and the narrative sequence that follows (V–XVII in §2). Readers will see that the complexity of the figure of Meed is difficult to overstate, and therefore the bulk of the work done in this chapter centers on her. For readers unfamiliar with the poem, I outline the narrative sequence that surrounds Meed. Then I turn a critical eye toward Meed's morality (§1.1) and the corruption of virtue and law (§1.2).

§1 Lost in Meed

The poem itself begins with a dream vision of "all the world's wealth and its woe" (Prologue, 10). All manner of men—anchorites, hermits, pilgrims, palmers, friars from all four orders, parish priests, pardoners, bishops, and cardinals—work and wander according to their worldly desires. The figure of Holy Church comes down to explain the meaning of this dream to the dreamer, Will. "See these people, / How busily they move about the maze? / Most of the people that pass through this earth / Are satisfied with success in this world; / The only heaven they think of is here" (I.5–9). Christians are so immersed in this world that they take the material and intellectual gifts intended for use in worshipping Truth and instead order them toward wealth, power, and pleasure. Will sees the wisdom in her remarks, but he

---

2. See false virtues on page 28.

has not yet recognized the speaker as Holy Church. When he asks her who she is, she seems irritated: "I am Holy Church," she says, "you ought to know me. / I received you at first and made you free. / Godparents pledged you to fulfill my bidding, / To believe in me and love me all of your life" (I.72–75). Will feels convicted by his own need to amend his life and begs of Holy Church, "Teach me no more of treasure, but tell me this, / Sainted lady, how may I save my soul" (I.79–80). Holy Church gives Will his first catechetical lesson in Truth's doctrine of charity.

If Truth is a treasure, Will understands that he must also recognize Falsehood ("Teach me the way to recognize Falsehood" (II.4). Holy Church's answer unfolds over the next three passus (II–IV) in a sustained meditation on the figure of "Lady" Meed. It will turn out that Meed is associated with Falsehood, but her identity is revealed gradually. When she first enters, she commands Will's attention by her wonderful clothing, trimmed in fur, crowned with a coronet, with the richest rings on all five fingers. ("Her raiment and riches ravished my heart. / Whose wife she was and her name I wanted to know" [II.16–17].) This is Meed. Although the word itself "meed" may concern either good or bad rewards, Holy Church leaves no room for ambiguity, siding Meed wholly on the bad. For Meed has hurt Holy Church many times through lies, slander, contradictory teaching, as one would expect of the daughter of Favel (i.e., deceit). Holy Church pits herself against Meed who "in the pope's palace is privy as I" (II.23). "I should be higher," Holy Church explains, "for I come from better stock" (II.30).

Meed is about to marry False. Invited to the wedding are Meed's kin—"all the rich retinue rooted in false living"—knights, clerics, jurors, summoners, sheriffs, their clerks, messengers of justice, bailiffs, businessmen, agents, purveyors, victualers, lawyers, and of course Simony and Civil (II.55). Simony announces the charter that would make the marriage between Meed and False official, which also turns over the territories of the kingdom to all those that follow False, Favel and Liar. Theology is angered by the marriage, arguing for the actual legitimacy of Meed as the daughter of her mother Amends. Theology demands that Meed's potential marriage to False be taken up in court—oddly not an ecclesiastic court but a secular one.

Meed is left alone at Westminster to face the King, but during her long wait she is at work bribing judges, clerics, the mayor, sheriffs, sergeants, all law enforcers, and even her confessor. When brought to trial before the

King, the King announces his inclination to forgive her despite the fact that "the longer I let you go the more your truthfulness lessens, / For you've never done worse than when you accepted False" (III.136–37). He proposes that instead she take the knight Conscience as her husband. Conscience objects vociferously, denouncing Meed—outing her as a prostitute, protesting that she is integral to the corruption of medieval institutions including the church and courts. Meed defends herself by outlining her potential good works—for meed is fitting reward of a king to his subjects, or of masters to their faithful servants, for the livelihood of minstrels, tutor scholars, priests, and craftsmen. Meed is playing with the ambiguity of her name, suggesting that meed plays a constructive, essential role in her world. Conscience retorts by highlighting the conflict between what he means by "meed" and what Meed means by "meed."[3]

At this impasse, the King commands Conscience to make peace with Meed. Conscience refuses, proclaiming that he obeys Reason only. The King has Reason fetched. As Conscience and Reason travel back to Westminster, Wisdom and Wit follow Reason. Conscience warns Reason not to heed them as "covetousness' servants" (IV.33). (Therefore Wisdom and Wit, too, have malleable meanings. Conscience directs Reason as a moral authority, but so too Conscience depends on Reason.) Reason arrives in time to deal with a new matter. Peace comes with a petition against Wrong, whom Peace accuses of a litany of crimes—adultery, fornication, theft, murder, violence, coercion. Wisdom, Wit, and Meed rally on the side of Wrong. But the King resists them. Meed turns to Peace, begging for mercy and presenting him with gold in an attempt to make amends. Peace is swayed, but the King is not. Meed "mourned and just looked miserable / Because all the people called her a cunning, common whore" (IV.160–61). Meed is arrested. The King, along with Conscience and Reason, condemns lawyers for Meed's influence over them: "Through your law, I believe, I've lost much revenue; / Meed and men of your skill have often blocked the truth. / But Reason will reckon with you as long as I reign / And judge you by this day as you have deserved" (IV.169–72). The King orders Conscience to fire all his officers and hire those that love Reason. The episode ends with Will waking.

---

3. Economou translates this difference between bad-meed and good-meed into "meed" and "merit." Economou attempts to do justice to Langland's decision in the C-version to contrast "meed" with "mercede." "Mercede" derives from *mercedem*, denoting pay or wages, and Langland's "mercede" is the first and only time recorded in English. This important addition to the C-version differs from the A-version and B-version, which ally both meanings under "meed" itself.

Will's Wanderings

§1.1 Meed's (Im)Morality

Sham virtue is inextricable from meed in Passus II–IV. I concentrate this study by looking to the figure of Meed, first in her identity as revealed progressively in her relationship to Holy Church, her kin, and her activities; next in the latent semantic conflict over the meaning of "meed" and therefore Meed's own moral possibilities; and then in her corruption of the sacrament of penance, illustrating the extent of her reach into the medieval church.

Meed's Lineage and Kin

Meed is first presented as an aristocrat:

> I looked to my left as the lady said
> And saw a woman wonderfully clothed.
> She was trimmed all in fur, the world's finest,
> And crowned with a coronet as good as the king's;
> On all five fingers were the richest rings
> Set with red rubies and other precious gems.
> Her robes were richer than I can describe,
> To talk of her attire I don't have time;
> Her raiment and riches ravished my heart. (II.8–16)[4]

"Lady" Meed is produced as an answer to Will's honest desire—to recognize Falsehood—but she also becomes a desired object in Will's unreformed habits of willing. Her raiment and riches appear to be the treasure that Will longs for, yet he recognizes that they may be an impediment to his salvation.

Meed's identity is revealed gradually. Holy Church introduces her to Will as her enemy. She describes Meed as a liar and a bastard:

> That is the maid Meed, who has hurt me many times
> And lied against my beloved who is called Loyalty
> And slanders him to the lords that keep all our laws,
> In the king's court and the commons' she contradicts my teaching,
> In the pope's palace is privy as I.
> But Truth's would she weren't for she's a bastard.
> Favel was her father who has a fickle tongue

---

4. Meed might be said to parallel Alice Perrers, an actual political figure in late medieval England. See Aers, "Class, Gender," 64–66; Baldwin, *Theme of Government*, 24–38; Ormrod, "Trials of Alice Perrers," 366–96; Selzer, "Topical Allegory," 257–67.

Two Guides for the Journey

> And seldom speaks truth unless it's a trick,
> And Meed takes after him, as men remark on kin:
> *Like father, like daughter.* (II.19–28)

It would seem that Holy Church as daughter of Truth is antithetical to Meed. Meed is a "bastard" of Favel, "*like father, like daughter.*"

Yet Holy Church does not share Meed's full genealogy with Will. (Later Will learns that Meed is also the daughter of Amends.) Understandably, Holy Church strives to distinguish herself from Meed: "I should be higher, for I come from better stock; / He that fathered me *filius dei* is named" (II.30–31). She explains,

> The man that loves me and follows my will
> Shall have grace a-plenty and a good end,
> And the man that loves Meed, I'll bet my life,
> Will lose for her love a morsel of charity. (II.34–37)

These two loves directed through these two figures produce these two final ends: heaven and hell (see also I.126–35). Holy Church offers parting guidance to Will: "Now I commend you to Christ and his pure mother, / And never load your conscience with coveting meed" (II.51–52).

The negative connotations of meed take life in those who are invited to Meed's wedding. From the entire country come *all* kinds of men that were Meed's kin—the list includes knights, clerics, other common people, jurors, summoners, sheriffs, their clerks, messengers of justice, bailiffs, businessmen, agents, purveyors, victualers, and lawyers (II.57–61). The catalogue of Meed's kin occupies several lines of poetry and signals the pervasiveness of this figure with the narrator commenting, "I can't keep count of the crowd that ran with Meed" (II.62). The list crescendoes with Simony and Civil: "But Simony and Civil and his jurymen / Were tightest with Meed it seemed of all men" (II.63–4).[5] Simony is trafficking in sacred things and Civil personifies civil law. Both the sacred and civil are bound up in kinship with Meed. The language of kinship indicates a sharing in "kind," what medieval theologians mean by "nature." It signals the ontological mark of likeness and affinity between Meed and her kin.[6]

---

5. Meed's chief retainers as Simony and Civil fit the standards for commonplace material for conventional venality satire. See Yunck, *Lineage of Lady Meed*, 294.

6. Kynde, translated Kind, means "nature" in Middle English, *MED* sense 8(a): "(a) Nature as a source of living things or a regulative force operating in the material world; — often personified; bi (of) ~, of qualities, abilities, etc.: by native endowment, inborn, innate; of branches: natural, not grafted." Kinship is developed over the course of the

Things look bleak for the moral possibilities of Meed as Simony reads the charter that would seal her marriage to False. Theology objects.[7] Theology speaks on behalf of Truth and adds to Holy Church's genealogy from the opening lines of the passus.

> Now sorrow to you,
> To work on such a wedding that would earn Truth's wrath;
> May your counsel come to woe before this match is made!
> Meed is legitimate, the daughter of Amends.
> Though Favel's her father and Fickle-tongue's his,
> Amends was her mother, in true men's view,
> And without her mother, Meed can't be married . . .
> That False is faithless, the fiend's his father,
> Born a bastard he was never truly begot.
> And Meed's legitimate, a maid of a good family,
> She could kiss the king as his true cousin. (II.117–23; 143–46)

Theology insists on the legitimacy of Meed as the daughter of Amends. Meed's connection to Amends may signal the most hopeful of possibilities for her, that she may fulfill the highest of elusive moral standards set up in the poem.[8] The meaning of "amend" could be to return what you owe, *redde quod debes*. Meed's lineage alone charts out the ambiguity of her moral possibilities. Her name reflects her ambivalency.

---

poem. See Davlin, "Spirituality of Piers Plowman," 23–40; White, *Nature and Salvation*. For more on Kind, see page 73.

7. This establishes a pattern of invocations of texts against others involving claims to justice. See Galloway, *Penn Commentary*, 1:269. The invocation is particularly acute in the A- and B-texts where Theology cites Luke 10:7 ("the workman is worthy of his hire") pointing to the controversies in late medieval culture over just wage. In the C-text, Theology's example of just reward alludes to St. Lawrence's dying words, in II.136: "no man bot treuthe."

8. The *Middle English Dictionary* gives several relevant definitions of "amenden": (1) (a) to remedy (a lack, a fault, a bad situation); correct, rectify, right (a wrong, an injustice, an error); (3) (a) to restore (sb.) to health, make well; cure (a disease, etc.); (b) to recover from illness, get well; (5) to make amends for (an offense, injuries, etc.); make restitution; (10) to change or alter (sth.), esp. for the better; change (one's) attitude, desire, etc. (11) *Ethics* (a) To mend one's ways; turn away from (sin); (12) *Theol.* (a) To save (souls, mankind); (b) to free or absolve (sb. from sin); forgive (sins); (c) to make amends or atone for (sin); (13) (a) To punish (a misdeed); (b) to discipline (a person); reprove, chastise.

Two Guides for the Journey

The Meaning of "Meed"

The semantic conflict over the meaning of "meed" itself, or "reward," comes to a head in Conscience's argument with Meed.[9] In this argument, the polarized meanings of "meed" or reward become clear. For there are bad rewards such as a reward for one's bad actions—a bribe. And there are good rewards such as a reward for one's good works—spiritual merit.

Conscience shows the negative connotations of the meaning of "meed" by detailing Meed's activities. His litany of charges against her are long.

> Conscience said to the king, "God forbid!
> Woe to me if I should wed such a wife!
> For her faith's frail and her speech is fickle
> And she makes men act amiss over and over.
> She's troubled many that trusted in her treasure;
> She teaches wives and widows to be wanton
> And draws to lechery those that love her gifts.
> She ruined [the King's] father, she and False together;
> She's poisoned popes and impaired Holy Church.
> By him that made me, there's no better bawd
> Though men search through heaven, hell, and earth.
> For she wiggles her tail and wags her tongue,
> As common as the cartway to every bum,
> To monks et al., even lepers in the hedges;
> Learned and rude, they lie with her as they please." (III.155–69)

Meed corrupts "those that love her gifts" and "trusted in her treasure." Her reach encompasses men and women, the King and the Pope, monks and lepers, learned and rude. She "wiggles her tail and wags her tongue," and in this clever pun on Meed's "lying" Conscience links her promiscuity and pathological lying. Not only is she an aristocrat and courtly lady, a patroness of the church, an essential figure to secular and ecclesiastical courts; she is also a producer of wanton and destructive desire, a prostitute. She is common to all men; she is all things to all men.[10]

---

9. The figure of Conscience is rather different than our modern understanding of "conscience." See MacIntyre, *Whose Justice?*, chapter 11; Potts, *Conscience in Medieval Philosophy*; Morgan, "The Meaning of Kind Wit, Conscience, and Reason," 351–58. Something like Thomas' own view of Conscience emerges in XXI–XXII after the christological passages of *Piers* that allow the recoupling of virtue and law.

10. In some sense the delineation of the many roles of the figure of Meed reaches a climax here. Prostitution names a relationship of manipulation primarily configured by the market economy, which diminishes the community's possibility for a shared vision of the common good.

Conscience goes on to show "such mastery has Meed over men with money" in the courts (with jurors, summoners, county sheriffs, prisoners, criminals, judges, bondsmen) and the church (with the bishop's people, the pope and provisors, bishops who can barely read, parsons and priests and their mistresses) (III.170–91). He details how she has the potential to corrupt institutions to the core:

> She deprives religion and gives it disorder.
> There's no city under the sun nor realm so rich
> Where she's praised and permitted that can last at all
> Without wars or disaster or wicked laws
> And covetous customs that destroy the commons. (III.202–6)

Of course, Meed objects. She argues for her usefulness when the times get tough ("when times become tough Meed can be helpful" in III.222). Whereas Conscience is unpragmatic when it comes to war, Meed gets things done:

> "Therefore, I counsel no king to take any counsel
> From Conscience if he wants to conquer a country.
> If I were king, Conscience would never be my constable
> Or marshal men in battle," said Meed.
> "But had I, Meed, been marshal over his men in France,
> I'd have laid my life on the line—no less a pledge—
> That he'd be lord of that land end to end
> And king of those people to his own kin's profit,
> The least brat of his blood a baron's peer." (III.253–61)

Meed befits all kinds of men—a king rewards his humble subjects; emperors, earls, and lords reward their servants; masters reward their servants; beggars, bondsmen, minstrels, master tutor scholars, priests, craftsmen, even the "pope and all prelates accept presents / And give meed to men to maintain their laws" (III.270–71). She displays the many positive meanings of her name—gifts, honors, wages, alms, mass pennies, compensation, payment for merchandise. She insists that the institutional church and present political order depend upon and need her. "There's no living man that doesn't love meed," she asserts, "And glad to grasp it, great lord or poor man" (III.281–82).[11]

---

11. Aers writes, "Time and again, Meed's networks are unequivocally located in the agents, institutions, practices, and relationships of the Catholic Church. She is at home in its ordained officials, its lawyers, its distribution of benefices, its practice of the sacrament of penance (central in the poet's religious vision), and in its institutions from parish to

Finally Conscience sharpens the distinction between the two potential meanings of "meed" at work in the poem by distinguishing between "meed" and "merit," *mede* and *mercede*. Rather than "meed" having a polarized set of offspring, bribery and beatitude, Conscience surrenders "the shared and highly paradoxical parent. The offspring were so mutually hostile that the bond between them has dissolved."[12] Now there are two separate meanings: "meed" is unmerited reward and "merit" is merited reward. In shortcutting the potentially positive meanings of "meed" altogether, Langland grants the uniform blackness of "meed"—a judgment that his portrait of Meed has done much to foster.[13]

In a last ditch effort, Meed quotes Scripture in her defense—Proverbs 22:9: *Honorem adquiret qui dat munera* (He that maketh presents shall purchase victory and honor). But Conscience finishes that scripture with relish: *Animam autem aufert accipientium* (But he carrieth away the souls of the receivers).[14]

Meed's False Amends

Meed shows her perfidy best as she and the friars corrupt the sacrament of penance.[15] Preceding her trial before the King, she spends her time giving rich gifts to judges and making promises of advancement to clerics.

> Then came a confessor cloaked as a friar,
> Speaking in mildest tones to Meed the maid:
> "Though laymen and the learned have both lain with you,
> And Falsehood's supported you these forty winters,
> I'll absolve you myself for a horse-load of wheat
> And even be your beadsman and work against Conscience
> Among the likes of kings, knights, and clerics." (III.38–44)

---

papacy" ("Class, Gender," 66). Aers would therefore criticize the idealized version of the church in Duffy's *Stripping of the Altars*. See Aers, "Altars of Power," 90–105, which is in turn engaged in Duffy's "Preface to the Second Edition," xxi.

12. Adams takes up the differences between the B-version (mede) and C-version (mede versus mercede), albeit serving his own semi-Pelagian reading of Langland, in "Mede and Mercede," 230.

13. Ibid., 220.

14. This repartee, and outstanding ambiguities that surround it, could be regarded as a heuristic for the entire poem itself. See Davlin, *A Game of Heuene*.

15. See Pearsall, "Introduction," 22–24, for a primer on the anti-fraternalism of this period.

This confessor pays no regard to her sins, but promises to absolve her and pledge his allegiance in exchange for a horse-load of wheat. The traditional components of the sacrament of penance—contrition, confession, and penance—will all be warped in Meed's favor. This corrupt friar asks for no contrition, her confession itself is anticipatorily absolved, the penance a horse-load of wheat. He requires no church context, no larger community, and no Christ. Meed jumps at the chance.

> Then Meed for her misdeeds kneeled before this man,
> Made confession of her sins shamelessly, I believe,
> Told him her tale and gave him a gold coin
> To be her beadsman and look after her affairs,
> Even subverting the work of Conscience among knights and clerks.
>   And [the friar] straightaway absolved her and said:
> "We've a window in progress costing us plenty;
> If you'd have this gable glazed and your name engraved on it
> We'll sing our Meed in masses and matins
> Solemnly and softly as for a sister of our order." (III.45–54)

The narrator Will senses that Meed confesses "shamelessly," confirming every indication that everything about this confession is amiss. In turn the friar sees a good opportunity when it comes his way—he tacks on to his offer a chance for Meed to glaze the window gable.

Meed reciprocates the friar's enthusiasm, promising to befriend him "as long as you love those lords that like lechery / And fault not their ladies that love the same" (III.57–58). In exchange for his promise to offer lecherous lords and ladies the same easy absolution, she will amend his building:

> I'll have your church roofed and build you a cloister,
> Have your walls washed and your windows glazed
> And pay those that paint and make pictures for you
> So that all men will say that I'm one of your order. (III.64–67)

Meed is bribing the friar, offering him "meed" in the wicked sense. At the same time she is offering him false "amends." Her lineage as the daughter of Amends, a connection that that once seemed so promising to Theology, appears to have proved not only ambivalent but also open to corruption.

At this point in the poem, an unidentified voice criticizes Meed's promises to falsely "amend." For such engravings are forbidden to all good people, "lest pride and worldly pomp be painted there" (III.70) fueling friars' greed (III.72). Rather we should give our money to the poor.

Langland's gloss on Meed's activities rounds off this remarkable exchange between Meed and friar, who are both already corrupt but in turn further each other's corruption. Nowhere is it more obvious how Meed affects the community, institution, and practices of the church. Langland revisits and expands the scope of the devastation wrought by corruption of the sacrament of penance in the concluding episode of the poem (XXI–XXII).

That Meed is at home in the church is doubly problematic—for what it says about Meed and what it says about the church. For there are additional questions emerging from Langland's use of personification allegory and agency—what *is* Meed and how does she act? Is she an independent corrupting force who actively deforms the virtue of others and of institutions? Or is she created through these interactions as a passive response to the opportunities other figures present her? James Simpson understands Meed as pointing to "a series of social institutions (the monarchy; the aristocracy; the papacy; schools and universities; the parish church; and guilds), in each of which 'Mede' (actually nothing substantial herself) is what defines the relations between participants in those institutions. So personification allegory, in Langland's hands, is necessarily raising questions about social institutions, since the concepts denoted by the personified words inevitably attach themselves to particular institutions."[16] According to this logic, and given all that we now know and understand about Meed, we see that she is the personification of human relations in the monarchy, the aristocracy, the market economy, the political sphere, the courts. Therefore Meed *is* what defines relationships within the medieval church. She is the personification of social bonds among Christians. Christians' social bonds are bound—or, more accurately, divided—by meed.

§1.2 Losing Law, Love, and Virtue

The long narrative sequence in Passus II–IV follows Meed from Holy Church's initial denunciation, through the ambiguities of her identity, to her final condemnation before the King. Throughout these passus we have witnessed that almost everything that encounters Meed becomes corrupted through her influence.

As meed permeates an entire social-political-ecclesial world in Passus II–IV, virtue appears in parodic and vitiated forms. The distortion of virtue

---

16. Simpson, *Introduction to the B-Text*, 50. See also Fowler, "Persons in the Creation of Social Bonds," in *Literary Character*, 95–133; Lees, "Gender and Exchange," 112–30.

in these passages is made more palpable by returning to the preceding material of the poem—the Prologue. The Prologue includes a brief account of the harmonious ordering of the church narrated by Conscience. Here virtue is identified with the founding of the church and the hinge on which the moral life—and by extension eternal life—pivots. Of course virtue is not an escapist eschatological strategy, but names what it would be to live a heavenly life on earth, a proleptic life. Conscience and Common Sense allude to an order in which we are led in both love and justice by the special laws of Christ the Ruler. Soon true virtue disappears from view.

Whereas this brief account allies virtue and law to Christ, the rest of the Prologue–IV considers what common life looks like without Christ. In these passages, competition thrives. Meed dominates both virtue and law by distorting both to serve her purposes. Justice is a stranger—Theology and Conscience petition for justice in its absence. So too Reason, Conscience, and the King call upon the virtues but have no idea how to embody them. Those who are driven by profit and exchange to their own advantage determine the law. Meed's attempt at penance is half-hearted, at best, and is undermined by her immediate reversion to her characteristic activity of substituting true amends for false.

First I turn to virtue in the Prologue (1), then to law coupled with virtue in the rest of the poem (2). Together these passus trace how a world dominated by meed produces parodic forms of both virtue and law. Neither the individuals nor institutions in these passus have the wherewithal to escape this miry mess. And Langland offers few conceptual resources for the poem's wanderer—or the poem's reader—to know how to go on.

Corrupted Cardinal Virtues

Virtues make their first appearance in the Prologue when Conscience comes to accuse those who have corrupted the church. First Conscience narrates the establishment of the church:

> Some of the power given Peter I perceived,
> To bind and unbind, as the book tells us,
> How he left it with love as our lord wished
> Among the four virtues, most virtuous of virtues
> That are called cardinal and on which the gate hinges

By which Christ in his kingdom closes off heaven.
(Prologue, 128–33)[17]

Conscience brings together the church, virtue, and an allusion to Matthew 16:18–19. In traditional exegesis, the gates of hell are vice and sin; the gate of heaven is the virtues.

Langland's use of the word "cardinal" bears the bond between etymology and ontology. Namely the word "cardinal," which derives from the Latin *cardo* ("hinge"), plays on the meaning of these virtues as the *hinges* upon which the gates of heaven open and close. Thomas elaborates the image in terms that suggest the source for this passage in *Piers Plowman*.[18] "The term cardinal is taken from *cardo*, 'the hinge on which a door turns, as in Proverbs [26:14], "As a door turns on its hinges, so does a sluggard on his bed." Therefore, we call those virtues cardinal on which a human way of life is founded, and through which as through a door one proceeds...'"[19] Conscience's coupling of the cardinal virtues and church through Christ signal what is essential for salvation. These virtues carry cardinal importance for heaven, Christ's Kingdom, and life in the church (Prologue, 132–33). The cardinal virtues are rooted in ecclesiology and oriented toward eschatology.

The cardinal importance of these virtues as the "most virtuous of virtues" is the telling result of their being left "with love" (Prologue, 130). Augustine is renowned in the virtue ethics tradition for his claim that the cardinal virtues themselves are forms of love.

> As to virtue leading us to a happy life, I hold virtue to be nothing else than perfect love of God. For the fourfold division of virtue I regard as taken from four forms of love. For these four virtues (would that all felt their influence in their minds as they have their names in their mouths!), I should have no hesitation in defining them: that *temperance* is love giving itself entirely to that which is loved; *fortitude* is love readily bearing all things for the sake of the loved object; *justice* is love serving only the loved object, and therefore ruling rightly; *prudence* is love distinguishing with sagacity between what hinders it and what helps it. The object of

---

17. The original reads, "of þe power that Peter hadde." Economou's revision, "some of the power that Peter had," effectively circumscribes the authority of the apostle and the papacy.

18. Galloway, *Penn Commentary*, 1:110–11.

19. Ibid. For more on Langland's treatment of *cardo*, see page 105.

this love is not anything but only God, the chief good, the highest wisdom, the perfect harmony.[20]

Although the standard conception of the four cardinal virtues would have them stand independent from love or God, Langland's and Augustine's are left "with love" (Langland) and whose object is "not anything but only God" (Augustine). They share a happy vision of the most virtuous of virtues "on which the gate hinges / By which Christ in his kingdom closes off heaven" (Prologue, 132–33).

Yet—"but"—Conscience continues:

> "But the cardinals at court that the name also claim
> And its power presume in their choosing a pope,
> That power from Peter I would never impugn,
> For in love and learning lies the great election;
> Don't contradict for Holy Church's sake," said Conscience.
> (Prologue, 134–38)

In the same breath, Conscience turns from the power given Peter to the cardinals who "its power presume." In "presuming" Peter's power, the cardinals lay an unrightful claim to it.[21] Their claim to this power is suspect, as was the power presumed by the cardinals in the Great Schism of 1378 resulting in the deeply problematic ecclesial politics that mark a church with two papal "courts," one in Avignon and one in Rome. With two popes both assuming that power from Peter, Conscience's counsel not to impugn this power "for Holy Church's sake" appears difficult to heed.

The cardinals who claim the same name as the virtues, or caught the same name, bear the brunt of Conscience's critique. Economou's "the cardinals at court that the name also claim" has a different connotation and wordplay than the original "þe Cardinales at Court þat caught han such a name" (Russell-Kane, Prologue, 134–36). Whereas Economou's translation suggests a merely unrightful declaration ("claim"), the original captures how language itself is open to corruption and full reappropriation when wrenched from its original context ("caught"). Conscience draws attention to the potentially varied use of language to signal the non-parity between the *cardinal* virtues and the *cardinals* at court. The cardinals are separated from virtue, despite claiming the same "virtue" for themselves.

---

20. Augustine, *On the Morals of the Catholic Church*, 15.25.

21. The *Middle English Dictionary* on "presumen": (1) (a) to undertake without warrant, take upon oneself; (3) to seize or hold without right, usurp.

The rift between the cardinal virtues and cardinals is profound. Indeed it is not until the end of *Piers Plowman* that the cardinal virtues appear once again. In Passus XXI, Grace gives Piers the seeds of the cardinal virtues and sows them in the human soul. Finally the church, virtue, and cardinals are reunited. But in the intervening passus between the Prologue and the end of the poem, the corrupted cardinals occupy Langland's attention. He paints the portrait of a church assimilated to the late medieval market, accommodated by avarice and associated with meed.

Meed's Perversion of Law

In the remainder of the Prologue through Passus IV, Langland devotes his attention to the accommodation of the church to the world and the profound impact that this has on virtue and every other genuine good. Because virtue seems so elusive in these passus, we might pick up another saving thread: law.

Although law may come across as a distraction from a study primarily focused on Langland's treatment of virtue, this is because the integral connection between virtue and law has become obscured to us. In the tradition of late medieval virtue ethics, law and virtue go hand in hand.[22] At the very least, law is intended to prohibit the most grievous of vices; at most, it gradually leads toward virtue. Therefore law can serve as an aid and help in cultivating virtue. Without virtue, however, law becomes unmoored from its due *telos* and instead serves lesser ends. Such law ceases to be "law." This has serious implications for communal forms of life. These consequences are displayed in Langland's treatment of Meed, which takes us through Passus II–IV once again. The complexity of Meed as a figure is especially evident in her relationship to law, for at times she seems to be related to legitimate secular law and at others she seems hostile to law altogether. Her general effect is to eschew reciprocity and indeed sever the bonds of community, undermining the basic definition of justice that becomes a refrain throughout the poem: *redde quod debes*.

Now that the cardinals and virtue parted ways in the ecclesial context as narrated in the previous section, Langland turns to the secular context to narrate the founding of the commonwealth.

---

22. Examples include ST 1.2.90–108; Aers, "Justice and Wage-Labor," in *Faith, Ethics, and Church*, 56–75; Hibbs, "The Pedagogy of Law and Virtue"; MacIntyre, "Natural Law as Subversive," 61–83.

> Then a king came there, led by the knighthood,
> Whose might it was that allowed him to rule.
> Then came Common Sense, and the clerics he made,
> And Conscience and Common Sense together with knighthood
> Devised that the commons supply all provisions.
> Common Sense and the commons contrived all the crafts
> And to most profit a plow they then made,
> To live by true labor while life on land lasts. (Prologue, 139–46)

Pearsall's version clarifies that the knighthood's might allows the king to rule: "Thenne cam ther a kyng, knyghthede him ladde, / Myght of tho men made hym to regne" (Prologue, 139–40).[23] Cooperating with knighthood, Conscience and Common Sense devise "that the commons supply all provisions," guided by "true labor while life on land lasts." It may help to illustrate what is happening by pointing to the conditions for just law— such law is a precept of reason, promulgated by one in rightful authority, directed toward the common good (ST 1-2.90). Here law is a precept of Conscience and Common Sense conjoined with knighthood, promulgated by an oligarchical king, and directed toward the common good.

> Then Common Sense spoke to the king and the commons,
> "Christ keep you and your kingdom, king,
> And grant you so lead your land that Loyalty love you
> And for your righteous rule be rewarded in heaven."
> (Prologue, 147–50)

Common Sense's wonderful alliteration directed to the king and commons connects Christ, the kingdom, the king, *and* leadership, land, Loyalty, love, *and* righteous rule and reward. Loyalty, or "Lewte" in Middle English, is difficult to translate into modern terms. In this context, it takes up questions related to justice.[24] Justice has to do with relations with one's neighbor (e.g., Aristotle, *Ethics*, v. ii. 1130b; Thomas, ST 2-2.58.5). To configure "Loyalty" in this way takes it up into a social whole and implicates it in a network of virtues. It assumes an especially positive cast in loving. It would seem possible that Loyalty's love prospers under righteous rule. Such

---

23. The power of the king rests on a contract with the knights. Contrast the B-version's "Myght of the communes" (Prologue, 113). The C-version is more amenable to the model provided in Watts, *Henry VI and the Politics of Kingship*.

24. Its definitions in the *Middle English Dictionary* include "(a) Uprightness, honorableness, honesty; truth; justice, fairness; (b) loyalty, faithfulness; (c) allegiance; (d) loyalty or uprightness personified." See Kean, "Love, Law, and Lewte," 254–57. Cf. Conscience's invocation of "justice" in Passus XXI.405–6.

a judgment would cast the king as not so far from Christ. In sum, it would seem that virtue is not so far from reach.

Conscience's next speech highlights the interconnectedness of law, love, and justice through the person of Christ. This is the first time that law is mentioned in the poem.

> Conscience to the clergy and the king said,
> "I am king, I'm a prince," you say, but neither perhaps one day.
> Oh, you who rule by the special laws of Christ the Ruler,
> To do it better, be as loving as you're just to the letter.
> You should dress naked justice in tenderness.
> So you may reap just as you've sown.
> If you seed love, may love be what you reap.[25] (Prologue, 151–57)

Yet Common Sense and Conscience speak with a seriousness that indicts them without their knowing it. (Are they early examples of what Scripture warns are *multi multa* who *sciunt & seipsos nesciunt* [XI.166]?) Just a few lines earlier, both Common Sense and Conscience are crucial agents in constructing an order that lacks Christ, despite their references to Him. They are complicit in this social arrangement even as they judge it.

Immediately Conscience and the king go into court, where law does not function as it ought within the social order. Law itself is absent from the figures and social institutions that ought to be ordered by it. There is no justice but lawyers "pleading the law for pennies or pounds / And not opening their lips once for love of our lord" (Prologue, 161–62).[26] The gift of language itself becomes a commodity. This point is sent home in a long fable that closes the Prologue, where language serves as the instrument for the ideological justification of social wrongs and violence (Prologue, 165–232). Such a social order prefigures Meed.

We first meet Meed through Holy Church, who is introduced in Passus I and introduces us to Meed in Passus II. Holy Church claims that Meed has "lied against my beloved who is called Loyalty / And slanders him to the lords that keep all our laws" (II.20–21). Indeed Meed's kin includes lawmen of all kinds. The effect of the long list illustrates her deep bond with all the

---

25. Conscience's speech is in Latin. In the C-version, Langland omits Conscience's own insistence from the B-version that the speech is in Latin, marking the gap between the "lered and lewed," namely, those who do and do not know Latin.

26. This is another distinctive emphasis of the C-Text due to its placement to doubly emphasize the connection between king and law. The B-Text postpones the lawyers and courts until after the fable at B-Text Prologue, 211–13, although its language evokes the same connection.

members of secular and ecclesiastical courts (II.57–63). The list crescendos in Simony and Civil, the "tightest with Meed it seemed of all men" (II.64). Of course Simony contravenes ecclesiastical law and Civil may be corrupted civil law. Simony and Civil not only support, but advance the case for Meed's marriage to False through the charter by Favel: "In the year of the devil this deed is sealed, In Sir Simony's presence and with Civil's leave" (II.114–15). These examples of lawless lawmen point to a breakdown of community, an allowance for individuals to assert their will as they please.

Upon hearing this, Theology becomes angered at Simony. He argues for the legitimacy of Meed as the daughter of Amends. And he invokes law to prove his point:

> And since man may merit God's meed on high
> So it seems especially right on earth
> That Meed may be wed to no man but Truth;
> And you've endowed her with False, shame on your law!
> For by lies you freely take your rewards.
> What you and the lawyers get brings nothing
> To Holy Church, and you just chew up charity. (II.134–40)

Theology suggests that Simony and Civil have created the conditions for corrupting Meed, when clearly she has potential for her good: "man may merit God's meed." He emphasizes the priority of heavenly reward over and against any earthly reward ("for by lies you freely take your rewards"). He condemns them, "you've endowed her with False, shame on your law!" He continues, "What you and the lawyers get brings nothing / To Holy Church, and you just chew up charity" (II.139–140). This is probably best understood as a perversion of Eucharistic imagery, therefore Theology culminates on a note of utmost gravity (cf. XIX.81–93, XX.403–8).

But are Simony and Civil corrupting Meed or is Meed corrupting Simony and Civil? Theology suggests that other forces are attempting to corrupt Meed. But it is also plausible that she is a corrupting force on them—Simony and Civil act for Meed's sake. Casting her as the source for corruption fits with Holy Church's initial judgment against Meed's activities. Langland offers readers reason to couple the judgments of Theology and Holy Church—both apparent but questionable authorities—to suggest that Simony and Civil are corrupting Meed *and* that Meed is corrupting Simony and Civil. Agency goes both ways in Langland's complex allegory.

Theology proves a puzzling figure by proposing that the legality of Meed's marriage be settled in court in London (II.147–54). Scholars continue to puzzle over this suggestion.[27] Meed's entourage conveniently understand this to mean the king's council at Westminster. Yet marriage disputes were properly a matter for ecclesiastical courts. Could Theology mean the Christian courts in London? Or are Meed's followers intentionally misunderstanding Theology? Regardless of Theology's meaning, the result is that Theology ultimately subjects Meed to the same corrupt forms of law that already legitimate her activities. Meed's entourage begins to celebrate, understanding Theology's demand for a legal ruling as an affirmation rather than a contest.[28]

Theology also drops another clue to Meed's identity: "Meed's legitimate, a maid of a good family, / She could kiss the king as his true cousin" (II.145–46). In her trial before the King, therefore, we should expect to encounter yet another puzzling figure: the King himself.[29] The King is Meed's kin. The King, exactly like Meed's entourage, also enjoys convenient understanding of law. He conceives it as a form of coercion to bend others to his will (II.209–19). The King, like Conscience and Common Sense, does not acknowledge the conditions of his own existence. He intends to force Meed into submission to his law without understanding Meed's influence over and through the law.

While Meed waits for her trial, coming to her comfort are judges, clerics, and a friar. In return for her favor, the judges promise that she may marry whomever she pleases "despite Conscience's tricks and trade" (III.20), the clerics promise "to do what you will as long as you live" (III.29), the friar absolves her despite her complete lack of contrition. They bend the law to Meed's own will. Meed goes on to beseech "the mayor / Both the sheriffs and sergeants, and all law enforcers" (III.77–78). The next fifty lines or so concern Meed's begging the mayor to show mercy in punishing abuses of money and to be open to bribery himself. As this exchange unfolds, the narrator moralizes about the corruption Meed supports and "it is as if the narrator were vying with Meed for the mayor's attention . . . The

---

27. Galloway, *Penn Commentary*, 1:271–2.

28. The C-version emphasizes anticipated celebration: "To wende with h[e]m to westminstre [the] weddyng to honoure" (Russell-Kane, C, II.177). A and B on the same: "to witnesse þis dede" (Schmidt, *Vision of Piers Plowman*, A, II.125 and B, II.161).

29 For Bloomfield, the King is a "multidimensional symbol but whose majesty can unite the religious, social, and psychological realms, with the social (and political) bearing the main emphasis" who may become "the just ruler and saviour-emperor" (*Piers Plowman as a Fourteenth-Century Apocalypse*, 113). But Langland implies many more limitations for an earthly King. See Aers, "Visionary Eschatology," 3–17.

narrator nearly drowns out Meed with his excoriations of the abuses she is supporting."[30]

Soon Law is personified. But Conscience narrates Meed's activities:

> By Jesus! she corrupts the judges with her jewels;
> She perjures herself and puts obstacles
> Before faith's coming forth, so thickly her florins fly;
> She bends the law and sets lovedays at will.
> On her loveday one loses what Loyalty might win—
> Confusion for the common man though he plead his case forever!
> Law is so haughty and hates to conclude;
> Without money or presents he pleases so few. (III.192–99)

In subordinating the common good to her own, Meed is antagonistic to communal forms of justice. She corrupts those practices and activities that would cultivate the virtues.[31] Instead she promotes "covetous customs that destroy the commons" (III.206). Naturally Meed responds to Conscience in a detailed and self-justifying rejoinder. Her response delineates her relationship with the law through her connection to the institutional church and to the present political order (III.220–82). Precisely because she *is* connected to the institutional church and present political order do we see that she has corrupted the very institutions that should be inimical to her.

Passus IV only makes more pressing the inadequacy of law under Meed's influence. The trial in the King's court goes badly wrong when Meed buys Peace in place of amends. What exactly reconciliation looks like is far from clear at this point in the poem (IV.91).[32] Langland puts into the mouth of a "wise one": "If [Wrong] makes amends, let him out on bail / Which can be pledged for his offense and buy him relief / And amend what's been misdone and so much the better" (IV.84–6).[33] Yet it is not clear whether readers can trust this speaker or this course of action, first and foremost because the language of bail and buying further reinscribes agents in the market

---

30. Galloway, *Penn Commentary*, note on lines 77–127, 1:299.

31. Lovedays were a peace-keeping practice, established for the settlement of disputes through amicable agreement. See Bennett, "The Mediaeval Loveday," 351–70.

32. Meed's bribery is the very corruption to which the lovedays were subject (see ibid.). This activity sheds light on Meed's genealogy, for between Theology's speech on her as the daughter of Amends in II.120 and her cooperation with Favel here, she is now rendered "False Amends."

33. The insufficiency of the forms of repentance, forgiveness, and absolution in these early episodes is treated by Deagman in "The Formation of Forgiveness in *Piers Plowman*," 273–97.

economy. Against the regnant version of law and loyalty is Reason's reconciliation of both in love (IV.133–45). Reason sees that the way forward will have to be an abandonment of meed. The King too comes to recognize this.

> The King then called Conscience and Reason into council
> And kept looking angrily over at Meed
> And scowled at the lawyers and spoke to them directly;
> "Through your law, I believe, I've lost much revenue;
> Meed and men of your skill have often blocked the truth.
> But Reason will reckon with you as long as I reign
> And judge you, by this day, as you have deserved.
> Meed will not bail you out, by Mary in heaven!
> I will have loyalty in my law and no more haggling
> And my law will be delivered by true and upright men."
> (IV.166–75)

The King's bringing together of love, law, and loyalty harkens back to the ontological unity set out in the Prologue. But at this point in the poem, there are numerous obstacles to achieving this unity. For one, Conscience attributed these to Christ in the Prologue, but He has made no such appearance here. For another, there is no attempt at explanation either by the King or Reason for how the ontological disarray amongst them in the intervening passus was overcome. Yet another, Conscience points out that "without the commons' help, / It's going to be hard, by my head, to bring this about / And lead your liege lords fairly and squarely" (IV.177–79). The King's invocation of law, love, and loyalty depends on his naive assumption that they can be brought together through an agent's own willing, without those exact forms of assistance that a medieval Christian is trained to expect: the sacraments and the church. This resolution cannot be forged without someone paying the price. And in Passus XX, Christ does just that.

§2 Between Meed and Charity

Looking back, in this first episode Meed dramatizes urgent questions about what the virtues look like in the maze of this world. Meed herself is produced by and produces a culture obsessed with the relentless drive toward profit. In such a world, relationships are dominated by exchange. Meed corrodes community. She corrupts those practices and institutions that would cultivate the virtues. She perverts law to her own purposes. Her all-pervasive influence undermines the communal nature and common good of community, the character of virtue, and the lawfulness of law. She leads those around her astray.

As the poem unfolds in Passus IV through XVIII, the hope for finding the virtues seems lost. In a sequence in Passus VIII, for example, Piers attempts to build a Christian polity but uses coercion to do so. His frustrations are potentially resolved by an imperative from Truth at the open of Passus IX. Truth appears to offer new and very real hope for justice in a model of strenuous ethical activity. Does this answer previously vexing questions? No. The solution baptizes rather than challenges the terms dictated by the market, assuming that the individualistic economic interests of the merchants can be reconciled and integrated to serve a genuine common good. This sidestepping of the limitations of humanity's powers under the bondage of sin ends in frustration. Truth's pardon is: "*Qui bona egerunt ibunt in vitam eternam; / Qui vero mala in ignem eternum*" (IX.288–89). Yet the pardon itself is an incomplete recitation of the Athanasian creed, one that involves a fuller profession informed by the life of Christ and his activity on our behalf. This reconciliation wrought for us by Christ is the grounds for any pardon. Without it any pardon is premature. Indeed, at this point in the poem those resources are unavailable precisely because Christ has not yet appeared. So the priest eviscerates this pardon lifted from the creed: "I can find no pardon, / But only 'Do well and have well and God shall have your soul'" (IX.290–91). In Will's mind, the priest has pit Do-well against prayer, penance, and pardon. Passus IX leaves the Piers, Priest, and Will bewildered and restless.

Will blunders onward.

> Thus robed in russet I roamed about
> All of a summer season in search of Do-well,
> And often asked the people I met
> If any one of them knew where Do-well roomed,
> And what kind of man he might be I asked of many men. (X.1–5)

The friars claim Do-well resides with them, but Will replies "*Contra*" understanding that the virtues are unlikely to dwell alongside habitual sin, Do-Evil. As he dreams, Will learns that "Do-well and Do-better and Do-best the third / Are three fair virtues and are not far to find" (X.76–77). But through successive encounters with Thought, Wit, Wit's wife Dame Study, Dame Study's cousin Clergy, and Clergy's wife Scripture, Will learns how little he knows about the virtues. Will's own frustrations and difficulties intensify as he encounters a cascade of figures who all give him their own incomplete or misguided definitions of the virtues.

Will despairs, following Fortune to the "land of longing and love" (XI.170) and giving into its temptations of *Concupiscentia carnis*, Covetousness-of-eyes, and Pride-of-perfect-living. Down the line he adopts the specious guides of Recklessness and Imaginative, both of whom also fail him. More likely, but also specious, guides of Patience and Active advise Will on the good life. Will finally turns to *Liberum Arbitrium* to ask, "I trust, as I hope, / You could tell and direct me to Charity, as I live?" (XVIII.1–2).[34] *Liberum Arbitrium* leads Will to the Tree of Charity growing in the human heart, an image set forth that still does not answer the deepest of Will's desires: Christ Himself.[35]

The absence of Christ Himself in the poem up to Passus XIX is made palpable in the stories of Christ in Passus XVIII and early XIX. These stories, embedded in one of Will's dream visions, recount Christ's attack on the Temple merchants, the promise of his Resurrection, and his handing over to the justices. Will wakes from these stories to find that he has been abandoned by *Liberum Arbitrium*. His loss is couched in unmistakably Augustinian terms, and indeed because the poet has already cited Augustine and Isidore as authorities in naming functions of the soul (XVI.198), we may understand *liberum arbitrium* in ways that Augustine allows. Such an understanding holds "*liberum arbitrium*" to denote the power to choose to do the good rather than evil, as a will attaining to its proper end. "Free will," by contrast, presumes the power to choose between a variety of alternatives. Here our protagonist has lost *liberum arbitrium*—Will/*voluntas* has lost the power to attain its proper end.[36] Readers may also find hints for Langland's eventual resolution as Augustine traces the way of new life for the redeemed soul: "By the law is the knowledge of sin; by faith is the obtaining of grace against sin; by grace is the healing of the soul from the

---

34. Economou's rendering of the text's *Liberum Arbitrium* as Free Will is problematic since the word choice evokes a host of Reformation and post-Reformation directions, assumptions, and debates. See Stump, "Aquinas's Account of Freedom," 203–22. All the better to note Langland's use of *Liberum Arbitrium* because the C-text was revised to include it here (XVIII.180).

35. Elizabeth Salter regards the Tree of Charity as an exemplar of "diagrammatic allegory." See Salter, "*Piers Plowman*: An Introduction," 120–22.

36. The loss of *liberum arbitrium* in Augustinian terms would contrast to a depiction of Will's volitional failures as "illuminating." See Zeeman, *Piers Plowman and the Medieval Discourse of Desire*, introduction and chapter 1.

harmful effect of sin; by the healing of the soul is freedom of the will [*liberum arbitrium*]; by freedom of the will is the love of righteousness; by the love of righteousness is the operation of the law."[37]

Without faith, grace, or healing, one's progress will be frustrated. Will's story will conform to the Augustinian model. While Will waits—and wanders, readers surmise—he is *graciously* led into his next encounter.

Drawn forth by the liturgical year, Will encounters Abraham, Moses, and Jesus the Samaritan. The answers to Will's quest for Do-well, Do-better, and Do-best culminate, and are transformed once again, in Faith, Hope, and Charity. Charity's definitive work finally enables "the way" for Will's wanderings in the wilderness. Will sees Jesus the Samaritan, who embodies the theological virtue of charity. Will sees the Samaritan's salvific work in the sacraments and his sacrifice on the cross. In this moment of Easter joy, Will is finally transformed, exhorting his wife and daughter:

> Arise, and go reverence God's resurrection,
> And creep on your knees to the cross and kiss it as a jewel
> And most rightfully as a relic, none richer on earth.
> For it bore God's blessed body for our good. (XX.473–76)[38]

---

37. Augustine, *De spiritu et littera* 30.52.

38. Creeping to the Cross is associated with the liturgy of the Triduum, especially on Good Friday with the veiling of the Crucifix. Duffy explains how the Cross was unveiled for the act of reverence: "Clergy and people then crept barefoot on their knees to kiss the foot of the cross, held by two ministers." This practice was targeted by Protestant reformers from the 1530s onwards. Duffy, *Stripping of the Altars*, 29.

3

The Way of Charity

WE REACH THE CLIMAX of the poem—and the ultimate goal of Will's quest—in the figure of the Samaritan. The Samaritan is the fullest revelation of human deification expressed in Christ's charity. The Samaritan serves as exemplar and teacher of the fundamental integrity between charity, the life made perfect in community, Christ, and the sacraments. The "way" of Charity begins here.

Before the Samaritan comes Will's encounter with Abraham (with Faith) and Moses (with Hope). They tell him more about the Trinity and the law, but as in the history of the covenant they are incomplete without their fulfillment in Christ and charity. The poem's excursus on only two of the three theological virtues begs for concrete display to come in the life, Passion, and Resurrection of the Incarnate Christ who embodies Charity.[1] The advent of Christ finally "completes" the Trinity.

Finally, then, Will encounters Christ the Samaritan who embodies Charity. Will witnesses the Samaritan's care for *semyuief*, or *semivivus*, a man half-alive. The Samaritan explains his salvific care for *semyuief* to Will in terms of the Church, sacraments, and virtues. He also offers doctrinal meditations on the Trinity, Incarnation, and creation to describe the new community of the Church enlivened by Charity. The Samaritan explains

1. This display really is to come in the C-Text, in which Will meets Abraham and Moses in XVIII before the Samaritan's salvific work in XIX and trial, Passion, Harrowing of Hell, and Resurrection in XX. The B-Text includes the life of Christ through Good Friday just before Will wakes up (B.XVI.160–66). The later placement of the Passion in the C-Text makes clear that the consequences of Christ's work for Will and for the community are linked with the fuller narration of the life and death of Christ.

that those who participate in the sacraments must eschew sin, embody forgiveness, and enact kindness. In sum, the virtues of faith, hope, and charity are given a home in the Church, fostered by sacramental and penitential practice. The work of God who is Charity works through charity to establish a community that *is* Charity. Langland simultaneously identifies and differentiates "charity," portraying these essential elements as parts of a whole rather than as discrete realities. Yet these multiple identifications exceed Will's own limited understanding.

As the poem progresses, Will struggles to internalize all of this. Not only can Will not quite understand—for here and in the passus ensuing he relies on others such as Faith and Conscience to interpret for him—but also it is not clear that Will *can* live into charity. In these final meditations Langland hints at Will's failure—and ours—to live into Charity. Will's wanderings and Langland's treatment of "virtue" are far from over as this chapter ends.

Following upon the heels of chapter 2, this chapter completes the span of virtue in *Piers*. It follows the sham, hollow semblance of virtue one finds in those habitually corrupted to the fullest revelation of human deification expressed in virtue as one finds in Christ's charity. This range of virtue is identical to Thomas' in chapter 1, but cannot be separated from the practices and community that give rise to that virtue. Charity, as Langland presents it, is wed to a network of others, bolstered by sacramental practices meant to cultivate it, and creates a kind community to sustain it. In his response, Will remains all too human. Once again Will fails to understand and fails in the desire to follow through. We see more clearly than ever that Will is not on a straightforward march from false virtue to true virtue. This chapter goes further by setting upon an explanation of why, despite the compelling witness of charity, true virtue exceeds his grasp.

In this chapter, the first section focuses on faith and hope without charity (§1), the second focuses on charity as embodied in the Samaritan (§2), the third describes the Christian community formed by charity (§3), and the fourth offers a set of penultimate conclusions (§4).

§1 These Three Remain: Faith, Hope, and . . .

This episode is set into motion by a telling transition: Will is abandoned by *Liberum Arbitrium*:

> With much noise that night I awoke almost frantic;
> In my soul and all my senses after *Liberum Arbitrium*
> I truly waited, but didn't know where he went.
> And then on Mid-lent Sunday I met with a man,
> As hoar as a hawthorn and Abraham he was called.
> (XVIII.179–83)

This Augustinian description indicates that Will is not able to attain his proper end—the answer to his framing quest throughout the poem regarding salvation and charity. He is not free to pursue virtue himself because of the sin to which he is beholden. Yet he cannot yet see sin because he has not yet encountered Christ.

The setting shifts to "Mid-lent Sunday"—from no specific orientation to time to the liturgical season of Lent. It moves Will into the penitential season of confession, contrition, and absolution. Will meets Abraham who is "with faith . . . I couldn't tell a lie, / A herald of arms before there was any law" (XVIII.185–86).[2] As a herald, Abraham/Faith is a forerunner to his lord, bearing his blazon—the Trinity—as he enters into the tournament. This role anticipates Hope who "scouts after a knight" (XIX.1) and eventually Jesus the Jouster (XX.14).

Will's meeting Abraham/Faith marks a significant shift in the poem from Will's own story to the history of the covenant. For Faith's story returns Will to the foundation of the world, where the persons of the Trinity "were never apart" (XVIII.190). Prior to any law were the persons of the Godhead. The Trinity is literally before all things. Faith expounds the doctrine of the Trinity to Will:

> God, who never had beginning but when he thought it good,
> Sent forth his Son as servant that time
> To occupy himself here till issue had sprung,
> Who are Charity's children and Holy Church the mother.
> Patriarchs and prophets and apostles were the children,
> And Christ, Christendom and all Christians, Holy Church—
> That betokens the Trinity and true belief. (XVIII.204–10)[3]

---

2. Pearsall marks the seminal text behind the association of Abraham with the fourth Sunday in Lent: Gal 4:22–23 (note to XVIII.182). This mid-Lent reading supported the tradition of allegorizing the Old Testament, and the allusion, personification, and speech in this episode all pay homage to that tradition.

3. Simpson works from the B-Text (XVI.261–67) where Langland uses "attached," "borgh," "daunger," "maynprise," "wed," and "wage." Such language has heavily legal connotations in fourteenth-century England. Simpson, *Introduction to the B-Text*, 195. One might note that these legal connotations, the interplay of characters, and the specific

The Way of Charity

The articles and mysteries of Faith are connected in an indissoluble bond that mirrors that of the Trinity itself. In light of the Trinity, Faith introduces the old law and the new:

> And he promised me more for myself and my children,
> Mercy for our misdeeds as many times
> As we wished and were willing to ask with mouth and heart.
> And then he sent me to see and said I should
> Worship him with both wine and bread
> At once on an altar in worship of the Trinity,
> And make sacrifice so—it stands for something;
> I believe that the same Lord intends to make a new law.
> (XVIII.258–65)

Faith rehearses the familiar details of his life from Genesis—the covenantal promise, Melchizedek's priestly office, also the sacrifice of Isaac, Isaac's circumcision—as "standing for something" to come. This is a prefiguration of the new law. Faith himself seeks the coming of Christ/Charity with that law (XVIII.265–69). Yet Faith's relationship to the new law, and how the virtues of faith and charity relate to the new law, is unclear at this point.

Faith does lead Will to a preliminary understanding. Faith tells Will that only Christ can deliver humanity from our present evils. Faith states,

> No pledge may pay for us
> And no man put up bail or bring us out of that danger;
> From the Devil's pound no bailsman may bring us home,
> Till he comes of whom I speak, Christ is his name,
> Who shall deliver us some day out of the Devil's power.
> And lay down a better pledge for us than we are all worth,
> And that is life for life. (XVIII.279–85)

Will finally glimpses the reality of sin.

> "Alas," I said, "that sin shall hinder for so long
> The might of God's mercy that might amend us all!"
> And wept for his words. (XVIII.287–89)

In his first flash of recognition, Will is overcome by his need for forgiveness. Will weeps. Will finally understands the harm that sin inflicts.[4]

---

mention that Christ will "wage" prefigures a specific depiction of the Atonement.

4. See Aers, *Salvation and Sin*, 99.

Next comes Hope moving in the same direction as Faith and Will. Hope introduces himself as a fellow seeker who has been given the law and searches for its completion:

> "I am *Spes*, a spy," he said, "and scout after a knight
> Who gave me a commandment on Mount Sinai
> To rule all realms with righteousness and reason.
> Look, obey the letter," he said, "in Latin and Hebrew;
> That what I say is truth let whoever it pleases see."
> "Is it sealed?" I said; "may one see your letters?"
> "No, it's not," he said, "I seek him who keeps the seal,
> Which is Christ and Christendom and cross hanged upon it."
> (XIX.1–8)

Hope's introductory speech draws upon battlefield language introduced by Faith, the herald. Hope is a "scout," a "spie" (Pearsall, XIX.1). The letter is open for all to see as a record of the covenant of the old law. It awaits the seal of Christ the King as the sovereign's final token of confirmation of the covenant, and in sealing it Christ thereby confirms and fulfills it.[5] We will learn that Christ is King, Knight, and Conqueror in one person through Langland's use of metaphorical imagery derived from extant Christian tradition (XXI.26–27).[6]

The law of Hope accords with "righteousness and reason," "in righte and in resoun" (Pearsall, XIX.4). This law is a striking contrast to the law of Meed in the first episode. That law, emerging out of the unchecked practices of the economy of meed, was in actuality a distortion of law that went against both righteousness and Reason. The reconciliation of ideals once anticipated by Reason in Passus IV (IV.133–45)—that Reason was powerless to provide on his own—is now given. This gift and its proclamation are remarkably public in contrast to the private transactions of Meed.[7]

Langland uses Will as a narrator to describe the law given to Hope that awaits fulfillment:

---

5. Pearsall's note to XIX.7.

6. Kirk argues that the concatenation of images of Christ in *Piers* serves a particular narration of salvation history. Comprised of "a multiplicity of discontinuous but complementary images and contexts," the poem offers a Christology distinct from the affective piety of the later Middle Ages. Kirk, "Langland's Narrative Christology," 23.

7. Ironically a "common" prostitute is engaged in a fundamentally "privatizing" activity. For an argument on the fruitfulness of the distinction between private and public, a morality that privatizes versus one that publicizes, see Taylor, *Sources of the Self,* Part II.

> "Let's see your letters," I said, "we could know the law."
> [Hope/Moses] plucked forth a letter patent, a piece of hard rock
> On which two words were written and glossed in this way:
> *Love God and thy neighbor.*
> This was the text truly, I took a very good look.
> The gloss was written gloriously with a gilt pen:
> *On these two commandments dependeth the whole law.*
> (XIX.11–15)

The fuller portrait of Christ's new law, prefigured but as yet unseen, depends on *love*.[8] The letter of Hope alludes to Matthew 22:

> But the Pharisees hearing that he had silenced the Sadducees, came together: And one of them, a doctor of the law, asked him, tempting him: Master, which is the greatest commandment in the law? Jesus said to him: *Thou shalt love the Lord thy God with thy whole heart, and with thy whole soul, and with thy whole mind.* This is the greatest and the first commandment. And the second is like to this: *Thou shalt love thy neighbor as thyself.* On these two commandments depend the whole law and the prophets. (Matt 22:34–40)[9]

Christ's formulation of the law in Matthew echoes through Hope's christological expectation in XIX. In waiting for the seal, Hope waits for Him Who is to come: Christ Himself.

The core of the new law is love. Christ, Langland, and Thomas all describe it as such. Hope's speech bringing together law and the virtues is akin to Thomas' own presentation of the unity of divine law and infused virtues. The virtue of hope brings together obedience to law and love of God, for in hoping in God we are encouraged to obey God's commandments and to love God.[10] Love of God, or charity, is at the heart of Christ's saving work. In Passus XIX, Will learns of law perfected in love.

---

8. Cf. Baldwin's *Theme of Government in Piers Plowman*, 66, for a dark view of Christ's relationship to law by explaining this allegory of the law of Christ without mentioning love.

9. Thomas cites Matt 22 as offering the two commandments (*praeceptis*) of charity and writes, "God and our neighbor are those with whom we are friends, but love of them includes the loving of charity, since we love both God and our neighbor, in so far as we love ourselves and our neighbor to love God, and this is to have charity" (ST 2.2.25.2.ad1). For my purposes, I think it fair to interpret Langland's "love" to exactly mean Thomas' "charity" when Langland writes of the love of God.

10. ST 2.2.17.8. Thomas stands firmly in the tradition of the unity of the virtues. Cf. John Duns Scotus, who held that the theological virtues were independent from one

§2 Charity Embodied

The action in the poem after the allusion to Matthew 22 takes its cue from Luke:

> Just then a lawyer stood up to test Jesus. "Teacher," he said, "what must I do to inherit eternal life?" He said to him, "What is written in the law? What do you read there?" He answered, "You shall love the Lord your God with all your heart, and with all your soul, and with all your strength, and with all your mind; and your neighbor as yourself. And Jesus said to him . . ." (Luke 10:25–28)

Jesus answers the lawyer with the parable of the Good Samaritan. Langland re-enacts this parable in the poem through the figures of the Good Samaritan and *semyuief*. The Good Samaritan is the culmination of Will's quest for salvation as the personification of Charity itself. Yet the figure of *semyuief* is taken up by Charity. *Semyuief* bears the devastating wounds of sin. At the same time as Langland presents the most bright of possibilities for Will's attaining charity, he undercuts these possibilities with a powerful representation of sin.

In *Piers*, the parable reads,

> And as we went on our way thus discussing this matter,
> We then saw a Samaritan come sitting on a mule,
> Riding very fast in the direction we were going,
> Coming from a country that men called Jericho;
> He jounced along fast as he could to a joust in Jerusalem.
> Both Abraham and *Spes* and he met together
> In a wild wilderness where thieves had bound
> A man and given him a very bad time, it seemed to me then;
> For he could neither step nor stand nor stir a foot or hands
> Nor help himself in any way, for he seemed *semyuief*,
> And as naked as a needle and no help about. (XIX.46–56)[11]

Ben Smith contrasts Langland's personification of charity in the Good Samaritan to conventional medieval interpretation of the allegory, underscoring

---

another. See Duns Scotus, *Quaestiones in IV lib. Sententiarum*, in *Duns Scotus on the Will and Morality*; cited in Wood, *Ockham on the Virtues*.

11. Russell-Kane's "wi[d]e wildernesse" (Russell-Kane, XIX.54) is "wilde" to Pearsall (Pearsall, XIX.52). Aers writes that Russell and Kane's change of text for their chosen manuscript (Huntington Library, MS Hm 143) is done for "no good reason." Instead, Aers follows Pearsall's edition here, retaining "wilde" instead of their conjecture, "wide." Aers, *Salvation and Sin*, 211 n. 59.

the singularity of Langland's treatment while remaining wholly orthodox. This is one of the few points where Langland's allegorical technique lends itself to the four levels of scriptural exegesis. Smith writes, "at least four thematic patterns may be seen to underlie the figurative progression in *Piers* from Abraham-Faith and Moses-*Spes* to the Good Samaritan: the fulfillment of the Old Law in the New; the perfection and operation of faith and hope through the operation of charity; the salvation of the just men of the old dispensation through the supreme act of charity, Christ's sacrificial offering of himself; and, finally, the salvation of mankind, not through his own efforts, but by the unearned gift of divine grace."[12] Langland finally brings various figurative patterns to their conclusion in the personification of charity in the Good Samaritan.

Alongside the Samaritan is *semyuief.* David Aers explains that Langland's allegory of the Samaritan and *semyuief* is couched well within Augustine's treatments of the parable and shares the similarities with much of medieval exegesis.[13] The tradition of which Langland is a part understands *semyuief*—a man bound, beaten, stripped, and left for dead—as representing all of humanity wounded by sin. The Samaritan enables readers to see what had not yet been represented even in the poem's preceding inventive representations of vice: the devastating ravages of sin.[14] Sin renders us *semyuief,* half-alive: "For he could neither step nor stand nor stir a food or hands / Nor help himself in any way" (XIX.54–55).

The figuration of sin in *semyuief* plays out in remarkable ways in Langland's treatment of Faith, Hope, and Charity. Faith and Hope do nothing without Charity.

> Faith had first sight of him, but he flew away
> And wouldn't come nearer him than the length of nine fields.
> Hope came hopping after, he who had bragged about
> How with Moses' commandment he had helped many men;
> But when this sick man came into sight, he drew himself aside
> And with dread then backed away from him and dared not go nearer.
> (XIX.57–62)

---

12. Smith, *Traditional Imagery of Charity,* chapter 4, esp. 81, 88–89.

13. Including Thomas, Nicholas of Gorran, Nicholas of Lyra, Denis the Carthusian. Aers, *Salvation and Sin,* 88–99.

14. Aers, *Salvation and Sin,* 100. On the skill of perception as relates to morality, see Murdoch, "The Sovereignty of Good over Other Concepts," 99–117; Hauerwas, *Vision and Virtue*; Blum, *Moral Perception and Particularity.*

In contrast, the Samaritan immediately catches sight of the man and flies to him.

> But as soon as the Samaritan caught sight of this poor man,
> He dismounted immediately and held on to the reins
> And went to this man to look at his wounds,
> And perceived by his pulse he was in danger of dying
> And unless he made a quick recovery he'd never get up,
> And unbuckled his bottles and opened both up. (XIX.63–68)

He soothes his wounds, anoints him, bandages him, and leads him to *lavacrum-lex-dei* (XIX.71).[15] The *lavacrum-lex-dei* is the "bath of the law of God," is baptism (Titus 3:5), but may also involve the laundry of penance, where the soul is washed and cleansed.[16]

The Samaritan's care proves distinctly sacramental for the salvation of *semyuief* with the vocabulary and imagery of baptism, penance, and Eucharist. Langland's description of "salvation" draws upon multiple meanings of the root "salve"—it is medical ointment, spiritual remedy, and the marking of one's baptism.[17] The Samaritan explains to Will,

> He'll not be saved without the blood of a child,
> A child that must be born of a maid,
> And with the blood of that child anointed and baptized.
> And though he stand up and take a step, he'll never get strong
> Till he has eaten all that child and drunk his blood,
> And moreover be poulticed with patience when temptations excite him,
> (For no man ever came this way that wasn't robbed,
> Except myself truly and those I love),
> And further unless they believe loyally in that little child,
> That his body will heal us all in the end. (XIX.84–93)

The sacraments entail a complement. For *semyuief* must "moreover be poulticed with patience when temptations excite him" (XIX.89). The work of the sacraments is complemented by, indeed completed by, virtue. The sacraments provide healing, the virtues relief. These bodily narrations

---

15. In the B-Text, *semyuief* is sent to *"Lex Christi, a graunge"* (B.XVII.72). That *Lex Christi* and *lavacrum-lex-dei* are interwoven is one of many connections made in the poem; however, as it stands the C-Text brings out another sacramental aspect of the Samaritan's care.

16. Pearsall, note to XIX.73.

17. *Middle English Dictionary*: "1(a) A medicinal ointment for external use; a medicine, remedy; also, an ointment taken internally; . . . (c) a spiritual or religious remedy; 2 An aromatic ointment used for baptism, preserving dead bodies, etc."

of the restorative work of the Samaritan and his sacraments disclose the manifold processes involved in *semyuief*'s and all wayfarers' full recovery. Such processes are necessarily incomplete in this life. The body is inherently vulnerable—open to threats, illness, and deterioration—and so too are our moral capacities. Not only are we vulnerable, we are wounded. That is why the Samaritan entrusts *semyuief* to the care of the inn, which houses the infirm throughout the lifelong process of gradual healing.

The Samaritan's speech stresses that the body, specifically the Incarnation, is needed for bodily healing. By this, Langland participates in the long tradition of asserting the fittingness of sensible signs for sensible creatures.[18] The Samaritan's emphasis in Passus XIX proves to be of more than passing relevance. The Samaritan proceeds to explain the same doctrines of the Church with bodily metaphors, in contrast to the abstractions in Faith's Trinity and Hope's love toward which Will was initially drawn. Even as the material world is transformed through gifts, it bears traces of meed. At the same time as the Samaritan highlights the necessity of redemption through the Word made Flesh and the busy world of getting and spending recedes in taking *semyuief* "six or seven miles away from the new market" (XIX.72), the Samaritan also pays for *semyuief*'s lodging. The Samaritan cares for *semyuief* by giving of his own material resources, resources as concrete as the physical assistance he provides the wounded *semyuief*. The sacraments entail the exchange of material gifts in charitable almsgiving and the social interaction of Christians.[19]

This episode enacts important configurations of agency. *Semyuief* will "be saved," be "anointed and baptized," "be poulticed," to be healed through his own standing, eating, and believing. Yet *semyuief*'s standing, eating, and believing are not possible without the preceding intervention by the Samaritan and the salvific power of the sacraments. Langland allegorizes *semyuief*'s and therefore our powerlessness to do the good without grace. Without grace, we are *semyuief*—half-alive as well as half-dead.

This construal of agency contrasts to the widely accepted interpretation that Langland is a semi-Pelagian.[20] Robert Adams claims that

---

18. Langland's reticence regarding potentially bloody and fleshy elaborations of the sacrament of Eucharist runs contrary to commonplace late medieval tradition. Aers, *Sanctifying Signs*, 45.

19. Crassons, *Claims of Poverty*, 66.

20. Adams, "Piers's Pardon and Langland's Semi-Pelagianism," 367–418; Smith, *Book of the Incipit*, 172–74. Cf. Aers' engagement with Adams, Smith, and others around this set of disagreements in *Salvation and Sin*.

Langland "strongly repudiates key elements of the authentic Augustinian position and tends to emphasize the role of free will so far as to overshadow any theoretical statements he may make about a need for the divine concursus in human decisions."[21] Rather "Langland believed fervently in man's obligation to do his very best (*facere quod in se est*) and in its guaranteed complement, divine acceptation."[22] What finally determines whether or not God's call is effective is freely chosen human behavior. But Adams generates this interpretation of Langland by skipping the episode involving *semyuief* (XIX.46–93) to focus on the Samaritan's conversation with Will about the mystery of the Godhead (e.g., XIX.182–91). Adams does not appear to be concerned here or anywhere else with the *semyuief* parable and its implications, including how its placement might transform the meaning of the accompanying reflections by the Samaritan.[23]

Rather the model of agency in Langland manifests in a depiction of *semyuief* who responds to the initiative of the Samaritan only because the Samaritan has enabled *semyuief* to do so. The activity is best figured as initially and finally on the Samaritan's side. The activity of the Samaritan affects sin and effects grace. Helpless *semyuief* must be borne into the Church described sacramentally: "*lavacrum-lex-dei*, a grange" (XIX.71), and given the resources he needs in order to be continually healed. Langland's account of agency is indebted to a specific doctrine of sin, Christology, ecclesiology, and theology of grace.

The eucharistic and baptismal imagery in the Samaritan's speech hints at an ideal that bears scrutiny. The imagery is indebted to a paradox of mutual indwelling: those to be healed both receive "that child and drunk his blood" within themselves by eating and drinking (XIX.88) and "with the blood of that child anointed and baptized" (XIX.86).[24] The healing process involves both a taking-into and an immersion-in. This description of the sacraments emphasizes *incorporation*—an ideal that is becoming increasingly eclipsed in this period. By the late Middle Ages, "the mass was becoming more and more of a spectacle and less and less of a communion. The emphasis was increasingly on watching Christ's body rather than be-

21. Adams, "Piers's Pardon," 371. Adams describes the tradition of the later Augustine as the "total depravity of the human will, double predestination completely uncaused, and grace that irresistibly leads the elect—and only the elect—to beatitude" (ibid., 383).

22. Ibid., 377.

23. Aers, *Salvation and Sin*, 84–88. Aers uses Adams and Coleman as entrees into a recovery of a robust Christology presented in Langland.

24. Davlin, *Place of God*, chapter 3. Cf. Simpson, *Introduction to the B-text*, 198.

ing incorporated in it."[25] Here corporate worship and participation in the sacraments come with the promise that "his body will heal us all in the end" (XIX.93).

Stepping back from the action of the poem for a moment, it can be useful to note Langland's command of language regarding the virtues. Langland first introduces the virtues in the Prologue of *Piers Plowman*: "left with love ... the four virtues, most virtuous of virtues / That are called cardinal and on which the gate hinges / By which Christ in his kingdom closes off heaven" (Prologue, 128–33). The next line follows: "But the cardinals at court that the name also claim" (Prologue, 134). In these lines, Langland implies two related uses of "virtue" with different meanings. The first meaning is connected to love, Christ, His kingdom, and heaven. The second meaning is linked with dark judgments regarding the so-called virtue of schismatic cardinals, who are condemned later.

Finally, the episode of this chapter, with Langland's re-figuration of the parable of the Good Samaritan, issues in a third and ultimate meaning of "virtue." Will encounters Charity in the Good Samaritan, a figure whose meaning is identical with his action. For Langland, all other meanings of "virtue" are subordinate to and refer to this reality of Charity embodied. In the Samaritan, we have the fullest and complete meaning of "Charity" specifically and "virtue" in general. Thus it would appear that —in tracing these saving strands throughout the poem—we come to appreciate how Langland shares with Thomas a theological understanding of "virtue" as an analogical term.

§3 Charity's Community

In more general terms, Kate Crassons writes that the Samaritan episode "clearly emphasizes the absolute centrality of baptism, penance, and the Eucharist for *semyuief's* health and rehabilitation. The mode in which the poem teaches this theological lesson is important, however. In retelling the Samaritan parable as an allegory of sacramental theology, the poem simultaneously constrains the allegorical dimensions of the episode to present the sacraments literally as a form of social relation constituted by one

---

25. Beckwith, *Christ's Body*, 36–37. Contrast idealized eucharistic celebration in Duffy, *Stripping of the Altars*, 91, and a correspondingly more social experience in Bossy, "The Mass as a Social Institution, 1200–1700," 29–61.

person's charitable aid of another."²⁶ The Samaritan segues seamlessly from this sacramental moment to the form of life that liturgy entails. Those who receive the sacraments are meant to live out the Gospel with two integral marks of that life: forgiveness and kindness. In the remainder of Passus XIX, the Samaritan discloses these social realities through the image of the Trinity.

The Samaritan begins with similes used to describe various relational models of the Trinity:

> For God who began all in the world's beginning
> Acted first as a first, and still is, as I believe,
> Holding the world in his hand. (XIX.111–13)²⁷

> For the Trinity is likened to a torch or a taper
> As if wax and a wick were twined together
> And then fire flaming forth from both. (XIX.167–69)

These examples are tentative attempts to concretize the abstract three-ness and unity of the Trinity. Yet the Samaritan himself acknowledges our limitations. All such undertakings will finally be futile, if it is true that God eludes attempts to finally name God.²⁸

The Samaritan weaves forgiveness into one of his descriptions of the Trinity:

> And as wax and nothing more upon a warm coal
> Will burn and blaze, if they're together
> And console those who, sitting in darkness cannot see,
> So will the Father forgive folk of mild heart
> Who ruefully repent and make restitution,
> Inasmuch as they can amend and repay. (XIX, 196–201)

---

26. Crassons, *Claims of Poverty*, 65.

27. Skeat suggests a possible original source for this image: Isa 40:12. Skeat, *Notes to "Piers the Plowman"*. It becomes a part of the hymn sung at matins in the service of the Blessed Virgin Mary and in the office of the Annunciation. Davlin notes the intertextual links with Will's quotation of Eccl 9:1 in B.10.429 and Piers' quotation of Ps 36:24 in B.16.25. Cf. Julian of Norwich, *Showings*, Revelation I, chapter 5.

28. Augustine concludes his book-long meditation on the doctrine of the Trinity thus: "A wise man was speaking of you in his book which is now called Sirach as its proper name, and he said, *We say many things and do not attain, and the sum of our words is, he is all things* (Sir 43:27). So when we do attain to you, there will be an end to these many things which we say and do not attain, and you will remain one, yet all in all" (*The Trinity*, epilogue [Hill, 444]).

The Way of Charity

The Samaritan explains that folk who forgive and are forgiven will receive the Father's mercy. They are to make restitution, to "amend and repay" (XIX.201). To amend and repay involves making restitution for one's debts of sin, a practice at the heart of the virtue of justice and the refrain of *redde quod debes* throughout the poem. In Passus II–IV, the language of "amend and repay" evidences especially problematic associations with economic exchange and support Meed's abuse of the sacrament of penance. (The refrain *redde quod debes* receives greater specificity in the sacrament of penance in the final passus, both in the language of Christ's salvific work and in the penitential demand tied to the sacrament of the altar. However much justice is of "cardinal" importance throughout the poem, its contours prove somewhat elusive.) In XIX the Samaritan speaks of real forgiveness. It requires that the sinner make good with the community by embodying Christ's witness.

The sacrament of reconciliation entails a life of "kindness." The Samaritan explores an etymological connection to illustrate an ontological one—kindness, kinship, and kind. The relationship amongst Christians and Christ is one of bodiliness and blood animated by the Holy Spirit, God's own kindness. Sharing in the Incarnate Christ's body and blood is a kinship with God (Kynde). Such kinship entails kindness to our fellow Christians. Kindness builds up love and charity, extending Christ's own doing. *Un*kindness destroys love and charity, undoes Christ's doing, and uncreates creation. Unkindness coupled with sacramental practice is futile ("The Holy Ghost won't hear you or help you, you can be sure. / For unkindness quenches him so that he can't shine / Or burn or blaze clear because of unkindness' blowing" [XIX.219–21]). Those who sever the sacramental practices from the kind of life those sacraments entail betray our kinship with Christ, our kind or nature.

In sum, the Samaritan's treatment of sacraments, church, and virtue earlier in Passus XIX open to later doctrinal extrapolation of the Trinity to include the Incarnation and all creation in kinship. The Samaritan's similes begin with the Three Persons and move to relations among human persons. This movement is part of the cosmic story extending the inner relationship of the Creator to all of creation.

Therefore the Samaritan's extension of the model of the Trinity entails that kind folks who are forgiven form a special kind of community. Langland's theology of sacraments is distinctly communal in its essence. This community is an ecclesial community founded in grace and enabled by the

Spirit and Christ to incorporate the outsider by way of the sacraments. Incorporation entails corporate practices. As the community is *corpus Christi*, its onus is to witness to Christ's virtues and Christ's practices, not the least of which is the love so powerfully demonstrated in the *semyuief* episode. All its communal practices—forgiveness, kindness, and charity—are inexhaustible. The community's identity must be constantly performed. *Piers Plowman* instructs on this point as the poem enacts the ostensible subject of its message. The Samaritan's activity shows the claims that the Samaritan is called upon to articulate for Will. This episode makes manifest the drama of living the Gospel and sets high stakes for the community predicated on the Samaritan's witness.

Once again, Will asks how he might be saved:

> "Suppose I had sinned so," I said, "and had to die now,
> And I'm now sorry I so offended the Holy Spirit,
> Confess myself and cry for his grace, God who made all,
> And mildly ask for his mercy, might I not be saved?"
> (XIX.274–77)

Will turns his driving question in the poem, "How may I save my soul?" (I.80) into a passive construction: "might I not be saved?" Will seems to recognize the limits of his own agency and will—an insight he ought to have derived from the figure of *semyuief*. The Samaritan responds: "Yes, provided you repent so / That through repentance righteousness might turn to pity" (XIX.278–79). The Samaritan brings together right living through the virtues and the sacraments to explain how Will can live into his salvation. This is the path to salvation for all travelers—a journey possible through the gracious assistance of the sacraments, confirmed in the virtues and sustained by a eucharistic community.

In sum, the work of the Samaritan allegorizes the process of recognition, forgiveness, and healing. The healing process that *semyuief* must undergo is exactly that—a process. For the sacraments of the Church are a salve that must be continually applied to the wounds of sin. All are in desperate need of healing, and "his body will heal us all in the end" (XIX, 93). This healing is bodily in character, where ours is effected only through "his body," the Eucharist. It is finally God Who finds a way to heal us. It is finally divine activity that saves us. The emphasis in XIX lands on God's forgiving kindness and our sin. The sin disclosed in connection to *semyuief* is carried into the Samaritan's account of community practice. The community requires the sacraments in order to maintain God's forgiving presence and kindness among them. Through the figures of the Samaritan and *semyuief,* Langland discloses the necessity of the sacraments and the Church, the gratuity of grace, and the centrality of charity for restoration of right relationships.

But in the same breath—XIX.280 and following—the Samaritan leaves open the possibility that accommodation to corrupt practices will enslave the will as it turns inward away from the grace given opening to full life in Christ. The work of Christ and the charity made possible by Him are integral to the life for which creatures were created. The stakes are high for living into this form of life made possible by Christ, for "to all unkind creatures, as Christ Himself witnesses, *Amen I say to you, I know you not*" (XIX.214). Do Will and *semyuief* now have the resources to live in charity?

§4 Conclusion Mid-Way

Chapters 2 and 3 attend to the extremes of virtue set out in Langland's poem—the corruption of communal forms of life and law as figured by Meed and the flourishing of charity in a kind community christened by Christ the Samaritan. Together these episodes cover our life's possibilities for virtue and map onto Thomas' possibilities within "imperfect beatitude" in chapter 1.

Yet the poem's presentation helps us better understand why it might not be so easy to locate oneself within this range. Moving through the labyrinthine poem between these extremes, we find that we are not quite disoriented, but more likely come to identify ourselves in and with the allegorical wandering Will. Will—the faculty of desire itself—runs in tandem with our own moral possibilities.

So far having met Meed and the Samaritan, what is possible for Will? Langland's answer does not allow us to focus on one figure alone. This is because Langland's vision of salvation is fundamentally social. It includes fulfilling the demand of justice, *redde quod debes* to others, as a condition for forgiveness, the sacrament of penance, and living in kindness. It depends upon the healing provided in the sacrament of eucharist, which signifies and causes unity with Christ and Christ's community. Living rightly with others on the way of charity *is* our salvation.

The concluding question is better put: what does Langland show us in the network of relationships surrounding Meed and the Samaritan? Meed acts in concert with the main figures of the poem—Will, Theology, the

King. At the beginning of Passus II, Will desires Meed as the treasure for which he longs. But Will also recognizes her as an impediment to salvation. Will is susceptible to her seduction because he does not yet have the powers of rightly ordered desire and rightly ordered intellect to rightly love Truth. Holy Church points Will in the right direction—heavenward—but leaves Will to search for the virtues in the remainder of Passus II–IV. Another promising figure, Theology, excludes himself from recognizing the possibility of the evils of Meed manifested socially. He seems to exclude one manifestation in particular: Meed's corrupting influence on the law. This is ironically the very measuring stick by which Theology exonerates the culpability of Meed as an individual. As a result of his misapprehension of the true law, Theology applies its corrupted counterfeit, leaving a legal loophole for Meed to escape justice. Like Theology, the King misapprehends the nature of the law and the evil nature of Meed. But unlike Theology, the King's misapprehension of the law is attributable to his own disordered desire. Rather the King's own desire to rule, to command, and even to forgive appears a result of his desire for dominion, recalling the dark satire from the Prologue. In each of these figures (Will, Theology, King), the elements of agency (desire, intellectual powers, the individual and social influence of Meed) all interact in remarkably different ways. Langland catalogues how *all* of our faculties, *all* of our relationships, are implicated in Meed's networks.

Turning to the Samaritan, Will's limitations come to the fore. Important as the Samaritan is—who is Charity and Christ—the ironic undercurrent is that Will struggles to recognize Him. His struggles to see this figure are of a piece with his earlier failure to recognize Holy Church in Passus II. In these latter passus, Will flounders through multiple identifications that are never quite fixed—of the Samaritan and Piers ("One who resembled the Samaritan and Piers the plowman somewhat," XX.8), Piers and Jesus ("very much in all his limbs like our Lord Jesus," XXI.8), Piers and Christ (narration by Conscience explicitly identifies Piers with Christ), the Samaritan and Christ (a Crucified Lord uses the language of the Samaritan). Will even struggles to identify Christ and Jesus.[29] No wonder—the presence of Christ is more mediated and more elusive than in other contemporary medieval

---

29. For example, in Passus XXI Will expresses confusion over whether what Conscience calls Christ is what Jews call Jesus. Earlier Faith clarified this, citing the Chalcedonian formula as explaining the two proper names in XX.21ff. Conscience tries to help Will by narrating one more life of Christ in XXI.62 onward.

texts.[30] Will's epistemic difficulties cast a shadow over this beautiful figuration of divine charity.

It is in this same context that Faith, Hope, and Will all fail *semyuief*. Faith flies away when he has first sight of him, "and wouldn't come nearer him than the length of nine fields" (XIX.58). Hope "drew himself aside / And with dread then backed away from him and dared not go nearer" (XIX.61–62). Will fails to see him throughout his wanderings in the wild wilderness. The three figures of Faith, Hope, and Will disclose to us our own resistance to see ourselves as wounded by sin. *We are semyuief.* We are half-alive, half-dead.

That we fail to recognize Christ is bound up in how we fail to recognize ourselves. Clarity regarding our continued enslavement to sin would at least allow us to anticipate our failure to embody the Samaritan's teachings on charity. It would also allow us to anticipate what comes next in Will's journey in XXI–XXII: the will's rebellion against the moral demands of the sacraments, the inexorability of epistemic ambiguity—in sum, "The wretch, concentred all in self."[31] Will's journey is far from finished when I leave off this chapter.

---

30. Aers, *Sanctifying Signs*, 47–48.
31. Scott, *Lay of the Last Minstrel*, Canto VI, Stanza 1.

4

Surprises Along the Way

CHARITY ENCOMPASSES THE ENTIRE way of virtue—its beginning, way, and end. But charity is not a path straight to God because, as Langland depicts poignantly through an allegorized lost Will, we are left wandering when guided by our ingrained patterns of sin. What kind of virtue remains for those of us whose habits of resistance frustrate our progress? Charity amid our weakness and failings is the subject of this chapter.

Charity stands as the most perfect of our necessarily imperfect virtues. Yet like the rest of our virtues, Thomas shows us in chapter 1, it lacks something of the full and total meaning of "virtue." These corresponding grades of (im)perfection draw on the logic of analogy, and can be used to develop the internal differentiation of charity. This chapter explores how Thomas' notion of perfect virtue includes a sense of incompletion and imperfection.

Charity is an unabashedly theological virtue. It is our initiation into and participation in the divine life. It concerns God directly. It is integrally related to all of our other virtues, and informs our understanding of Thomas' common distinction between the acquired and infused virtues (§1). As we go on, we find surprises along the way, hence the title of this chapter. We find that Thomas' treatment of charity likens it as to an *acquired* habit that always inclines to its greater perfection (§2). Therefore charity appears closer to the other virtues than his scheme admits at first look. Thomas also seems to question the strict distinction between acquired and infused virtue from the other way around. He holds that charity is the form of the virtues, alongside his thesis that "virtue" is an analogical term. Together these twin theses inform the surprisingly *theological* character of acquired virtue (§3). This theological rendering of acquired virtue through charity enables the acquired virtues to reach their true destiny.

§1 The Acquired and Infused Virtues

First we turn to Thomas' well-known and often-used distinction between acquired and infused virtues.[1] In Thomas' first question on the virtues, Thomas introduces the acquired virtues. He depends heavily on Aristotle and Augustine for his account of virtues. For example, he gives his support to Augustine's definition: "Virtue is a good quality of mind by which one lives righteously, of which no one can make bad use, which God works in us without us."[2] Yet Thomas actually modifies both Aristotle and Augustine in his treatment of the acquired virtues:

> Now the *efficient* cause of infused virtue, which is what is being defined here, is God. For this reason, the definition says, "which God works in us without us." And if this part is left out, then the rest of the definition will be common to all virtues, both acquired and infused. (ST 1-2.55.4)

In building the distinction between "acquired" and "infused" into his definition of virtue, he affirms his inheritance from the main school of theological thought while at the same time developing his own thought within that definition.[3] Later in Question 63, he sharpens the difference between

---

1. I bracket relevant discussions on the role of acquired virtue in the life of a Christian. I am most sympathetic with the arguments that account for the continued role of acquired virtues in the life of a Christian—a reading both indebted to the history of interpretation of the *Summa* and the predominant interpretation today. Besides the prominent works by Osborne and Cessario, one may include Herdt, Inglis, Kent, Miner, and Sherwin. Challenges to the role of the acquired virtues in the life of a Christian include William C. Mattison III and Angela McKay Knobel. See Mattison's "Can Christians Possess the Acquired Cardinal Virtues?" and Knobel's "Infused and Acquired Virtues in Aquinas' Moral Philosophy," "Prudence and Acquired Moral Virtue," "Can the Infused and Acquired Virtues Coexist in the Christian Life?," "Two Theories of Christian Virtue," and "Relating Aquinas's Infused and Acquired Virtues."

2. ST 1-2.55.4.obj 1. Thomas takes himself to be quoting Augustine. Jordan argues "Thomas knows" this definition is "a conflation of Augustinian texts and especially of passages from *On Free Choice* 2, which supplies the middle clause of the Lombard's definition" derived from Peter Lombard's *Sentences* (*Rewritten Theology*, 159).

3. In his introduction to vol. 23 of the *Summa*, W. D. Hughes argues that the main school of thought is well represented by William of Auxerre, who held that the only true virtues are those which God works *in nobis sine nobis* (xxii). Inglis argues that the

acquired virtue and infused virtue—the acquired are "ordered toward a good that is regulated by the rule of human reason" and "can be caused by human acts insofar as those acts proceed from reason" whereas infused are "regulated by God's law and not by human reason" and "cannot be caused by human acts, whose principle is reason, but is instead caused in us solely by God's action" (ST 1-2.63.2). Acquired and infused virtues differ with respect to their origin, development, and end. He holds that moral virtues may be acquired or infused whereas the theological virtues are exclusively infused—effectively interchanging the earlier categorization of moral and theological virtues into acquired and infused virtues (ST 1-2.63.2–4).

Thomas adds an important third kind of virtue that develops the acquired and infused distinction: infused moral virtue.[4] He writes,

> Insofar as the moral virtues do what is good in relation to an end that does not exceed natural power, they can be acquired through human actions. And in this sense they can exist without charity, as they did in many Gentiles. However, insofar as the moral virtues do what is good in relation to our supernatural end, then in this sense they have the character of virtue perfectly and truly, and they are infused by God and cannot be acquired by human acts. And moral virtues of this sort cannot exist without charity. (ST 1-2.65.2)

This new third kind of virtue affords a *new* difference—between acquired moral virtue and infused moral virtue—rather than acquired virtue versus infused virtue. These important and crucial distinctions between the kinds of virtue correspond to different grades of perfection of the human person.

Important as these distinctions are, Thomas creatively undercuts any latent tendency to dichotomize our experience. He does this by presenting a complex portrait of charity with respect to the acquired and infused virtues.

---

preceding treatment of *in nobis sine nobis* by William Peraldus in his *Summa de vitiis et virtutibus* informed Thomas' treatment of the same and thus both "parted from the received Augustinian picture by interpreting this phrase as applicable only to infused virtue and not to the virtues that involve voluntary habit" ("Aquinas's Replication," 9).

4. ST 1-2.63.3 et ad2 shows Thomas' reasoning for the existence of infused moral virtue.

§2 The "Acquired" Infused Virtues

This section pursues a dual aim. The first aim is to follow the work of Thomas' first question on charity (Question 23) in iterating the integral character of "virtue" and "beatitude" while specifying that character further, beginning to account for charity's relationship to the other virtues, developing Thomas' complex account of divine-human agency, and even briefly reaching into Question 24 following Thomas' theses that even the perfect may progress. The second aim is to argue for the peculiar character of infused virtues. The infused virtues are unlike the acquired virtues in that they lack the *delectatio* or delight natural to acquired. Surprisingly like the acquired virtues, however, the infused must be further developed in order for us to make progress along the way. The virtue that makes this possible is charity.

Thomas comes to charity in the *Secunda Secundae* by following the biblical sequence of 1 Corinthians 13:13, starting first with faith, then hope, then love.[5] He begins with 1 Corinthians 13:12: "We see now through a glass in a dark manner; but then face to face," which for the wayfarer describes the initial ordering of the mind to God which is called faith (ST 2-2.1.5). Faith names the beginning of the journey whereby eternal life is begun in us (ST 2-2.4.1). Its object includes the mystery of Christ's Incarnation and Passion as the "way" by which we obtain beatitude (ST 2-2.2.7; 2-2.18.3). Faith is not an individual achievement, but a gift given to the community of the Church that communicates this gift in its sacraments. Next Thomas treats the entering of eternal happiness into the heart of the wayfarer such that a movement towards it arises—this movement being hope itself (ST 2-2.17.2.ad1). Hope is crucial to sustain movement back to God, for it sustains the presence of the ultimate end throughout the journey.

Despite appearances, Thomas' systematic interrelations between faith, hope, and love defy a single sequential ordering. Faith and hope both lead to charity, but also presuppose charity (ST 1-2.65.5; 2-2.4.7; 2-2.17.8). In terms of their relations, faith and hope are taken a step further in charity.

---

5. Langland's account of the virtues in his re-figuration of the parable of the Good Samaritan is amenable to these interrelationships between faith, hope, and charity—that faith and hope are incomplete without charity, that charity alone enables meritorious works, that charity entails friendship with God and neighbor. Langland adds at least three aspects to their shared understanding of charity: (1) Langland clarifies the christological figuration of charity, (2) Langland takes up *semyuief* alongside charity to allegorize his understanding of human agency and grace, and (3) Langland has Will run after Faith and Hope, all pursuing the Samaritan as the "right way" (XIX.77).

Thomas thinks of charity as the union between the human being and the God of his faith and hope.[6] Faith and Hope are ways God gives Godself to be known—under the determinative aspects of Faith as first truth and Hope as powerful aid—whereas Charity aims at God without restriction on God. Charity "attains God himself."[7] In charity, human beings now surpass themselves by participation in the Triune life. Charity alone remains in glory (ST 1-2.67.6). Charity alone makes other virtues what they are.

The language Thomas uses to describe charity expresses God's longing for his people in the intimacy characteristic of friendship: *convivere, conversatio, communicatio* (ST 2-2.23.1).[8] His language bears close attention, especially his careful use of *communicatio*.[9] Divine charity is ours in "a communication between the human and God, inasmuch as he communicates his beatitude to us" (ST 2-2.23.1). This "communication" is described in Scripture: "St. Paul refers to it, *God is faithful by whom you were called into the fellowship of his Son*." This *communicatio* is God's and as such calls into being a genuine fellowship impossible apart from it. It springs from God's desire. And it is uniquely transformative. This same *communicatio* marks the mystery of the Incarnation and calls creatures into the fullness of the Triune life. Thus charity qualifies the very faculty it has had "a hand" in making. Unlike the other virtues—temperance, for example, which perfects the sensuous appetite, or justice, which perfects the will—charity creates its own reception.

In a happy confluence of charity, beatitude, and *communicatio*, Thomas recalls his earlier treatment of beatitude in the questions on beatitude.[10] Both treatments affirm that God is the end of all beatitude and God is beatitude's way. The principle of beatitude, God, is charity (ST 2-2.26.1). Wadell suggests that when Thomas thinks about happiness in light of charity, "his

---

6. Schockenhoff, "Die Liebe als Freundschaft," 238.

7. ST 2-2.23.6, which Schockenhoff renders "Die Liebe erreicht Gott, wie er in sich selbst ist" (ibid.).

8. Cf. *societas, convivere, et conversatio* in *In III sent.*, 32.2. The etymological connection between these characteristics is instructive—living together, speaking with one another—and may show the integral bond between the realities of community and communication through communion.

9. See Schockenhoff, "Theological Virtue of Charity," 246–48 for the explanation that this is a substantive revision from Thomas' treatment of friendship in *The Commentary on the Sentences* (*In III Sent.*, 27.2.1). As the first medieval theologian to bring the Aristotelian idea of friendship to bear on analysis of God's charity, Thomas had to give up quite a bit from this line of thought to synthesize it with Christian doctrine.

10. See the section beginning on page 18.

conclusion is not only that we are most happy in God, but, more pointedly, that we cannot be happy unless we are friends of God. If God is our happiness, to whatever extent we have happiness we must have God. The difference, though subtle, is important because when Thomas thinks of happiness in terms of charity he sees the happiness of God not as something that awaits us at the end of a life of other types of happiness, but as precisely that from which all happiness flows."[11] Charity is the activity of God's sharing God's beatitude in friendship.

For all of that, charity is *ours*.[12] For it is something created in the soul. Charity arises from the inner principle infused into the created structure of the human being, obviating the idea that the Holy Spirit moves the mind as if by an extrinsic power. Equally unpalatable is the idea that the Holy Spirit moves the will as if it were an instrument. Rather, the will actuates its own effectiveness. Charity, like all other virtues, proceeds from habit: "therefore it is most necessary that, for us to perform the act of charity, there should be in us some habitual form superadded to the natural power, inclining that power to the act of charity, and causing it to act readily and with delight" (ST 2-2.23.2). Acting "readily" and "with delight," *prompte et delectabiliter*, is Thomas' naming of charity as a kind of pull rather than push. Thomas searches for the conceptual resources to depict charity as the good use of *pondus meum amor meum*—a *pondus* directed toward God of which Augustine writes.

Charity is singular and as such, is singularly important for the other virtues. Take the infused moral virtues. The infused moral virtues complicate Thomas' relationship to Aristotle on habit. By definition as "infused," they are from God; as "virtues," they are habits marked by perfected readiness and delight. Yet there opens a gap between the way in which infused moral virtues and the acquired moral virtues operate. The problem is that the infused moral virtues give an intrinsic facility without always excluding the extrinsic obstacles, whereas the acquired virtues exclude these extrinsic

---

11. Wadell, *Friends of God*, 17.

12. Cf. Thomas' argument for the power to know and love rightly in the Holy Spirit, a gift that becomes *ours* in ST 1.38 yet remains distinct. So Thomas does not hold, as Lombard does, that charity is nothing more than the Holy Spirit. Wadell treats Thomas' usage as highlighting two distinct senses of charity: one as the virtue expressive of active friendship with God and the other as the Spirit expressive of that friendship's perfection (*Friends of God*, 23). Wadell also treats the connections between the virtues and gifts, esp. 121–39.

obstacles by the repetition of acts.[13] Because of these standing impediments, the infused moral virtues may be difficult to act upon. Being marked by perfected readiness and delight—*prompte et delectabiliter*—are precisely characteristics that the infused virtues may *lack*.[14] Thomas pinpoints this contrast:

> It sometimes happens that someone who has a habit experiences difficulty in acting and, as a result, does not feel any pleasure or satisfaction in his act, and this because of some impediment that comes from the outside—as when someone who has the habit of a type of scientific knowledge experiences difficulty in understanding because of drowsiness or because of some sickness. Similarly, habits of the infused virtues sometimes experience difficulty in acting because of certain contrary dispositions that are left over from previous acts. This sort of difficulty does not occur in the same way in the case of the acquired moral virtues, because contrary dispositions are removed through the exercise of the acts by which those virtues are acquired. (ST 1-2.65.3.ad2)

Initially the other infused virtues lack the defining characteristic of the acquired: *delectatio*.[15] Expounding upon this same contrast, Schockenhoff writes,

> The efficacy of divine grace in the psychological structures of the human is not immediately given as a mental quality . . . Precisely the "*delectatio*" of virtue is still not the case . . . ["*Virtus infusa*"] are not given the motivating power of good as an experience of joy; at least in the beginning actions arising from mere "*virtus infusa*" must make do without the "*delectatio*" that belongs to acquired virtue.[16]

Therefore the infused virtues lack this perfection that the acquired already enjoy. (In turn, the acquired virtues lack the inner-directedness to the

---

13. Garrigou-Lagrange, *Three Ages of the Interior Life*, 62–63.

14. In this respect, the infused virtues are unlike the acquired virtues. Bonnie Kent notes that Thomas departs from an initial Aristotelian vein ("Habits and Virtues," 224–26, citing ST 1-2.51.4). Kent does not go far enough, however, in reckoning the difficulties that this later addition of infused habits introduces to Thomas' initial definition.

15. Schockenhoff notes the same in *Bonum hominis*, 291–320. I have little to add to Schockenhoff's magisterial treatment. A small curiosity, however, is Schockenhoff's treatment of *virtus infusa* coming before *virtus acquisita* even as he aims to follow Thomas' own movement through the "organic" process of virtue (ibid., 554 n. 289).

16. Ibid., 312–13.

ultimate end that the infused enjoy.) Infused virtue invokes a kind of non-habituated-ness—a characteristic noted in secondary scholarship.[17]

Going a step further, one may observe that this lack actually *likens* infused virtues to acquired virtues. That is, both acquired and infused virtues are in some sense incomplete. One might say that both are incomplete, though differently. The incompleteness of the infused indicates a gradual, rather than instantaneous, acquiescence to the movement of grace. Until it is moved by the *delectatio* of acquired virtue, infused virtue remains incomplete.

Without the ease of operation that properly characterizes a habit, the infused virtues concern the struggle for self-mastery rather than character. The infused virtues alone render a person self-controlled or continent rather than virtuous.[18] Robert Sokolowski observes:

> This contrast of the two kinds of virtue, the natural and the theological, is often the theme of literary treatments of Christianity. Very often such works will describe someone who is weak in self-control, someone who cannot master the inclination to alcohol or to sensuality, but who struggles with these inclinations and in this struggle still serves as an example of faith, hope, and charity. The very paradox of combining weakness with theological virtue in the same agent is a literary device that writers could not possibly resist, especially writers who live within the axioms of modernity.[19]

The problem is this: "although a good moral action is possible without any habitus in the power from which it proceeds, a moral *life* is not."[20]

At this point the term "infused virtues" may appear puzzling—namely as virtues that are not fully virtues—but this is not accidental.[21] One may explain this through affirming an analogical understanding of "virtue." In such a case, only exemplar virtue is the total, complete, absolute, perfect meaning of "virtue." Naturally the infused virtues do not invoke the same meaning. Yet a *new* notion attends charity: that infused virtue becomes

---

17. See Dell'Olio, *Foundations of Moral Selfhood*, 138; Inglis, "Aquinas's Replication," 3–27; Kent, "Habits and Virtues"; Porter, "Subversion of Virtue," 30–33.

18. Sokolowski, *God of Faith and Reason*, 75–80.

19. Ibid., 76. See Sherwin's "Infused Virtue and the Effects of Acquired Vice."

20. Finili, "On the Virtue of Religion," 85.

21. For example, Kent notes Odon Lottin's "admirably candid reservations" about Thomas' positing of the infused moral virtues in *Principes de morale*, 213–25, contrasting Lottin's forthrightness with many twentieth-century authors who either ignore or pass over this aspect of Thomas' ethics. Kent, "Habits and Virtues," 243 n. 32.

more fully "virtue" as it becomes more fully habituated. Charity is key. Charity, the first among virtues, already operates readily and with delight. It renders the other infused virtues perfect (ST 2-2.23.2). Charity inclines and delights in a movement that Thomas follows from virtues to gifts, for the perfection of the virtues is named in the gifts of the Spirit.[22]

Only as God moves us may charity move the rest of the virtues toward perfection. The perfection of the infused virtues relies most fundamentally on their being moved by charity. Thomas attempts to name the diverse elements of a complex account of agency—the result of our entering into a perfecting friendship with Charity Itself—in 2-2.23.2. In that article's *sed contra*, Thomas affirms Augustine's *De Doctrina Christiana*: "By charity I mean the movement of the soul towards the enjoyment of God for his own sake. But a movement of the soul is something created in the soul. Therefore charity is something created in the soul." Thomas' gloss draws upon *motio* vocabulary and implies the language of causation. This double invocation makes it clear that only God can bring about such an effect. Arguably Thomas articulates the work of charity in terms of "motion" and "causation" to articulate a new and more robust account of agency at the heart of the increasing perfection of the creature. In the *Summa*, "motion" is most often invoked in transgeneric relations, primarily between the Holy Spirit and creature whereas "causation" is most often reserved for describing intergeneric activity. Because charity becomes fully creatures' own (though we do not possess it perfectly), the language of causation becomes appropriate in addition to motion. Causation is possible because God's charity becomes creatures' own. His careful use of language serves as a warning against overarching explanations offered by any one idiom, sensitive to the difficulties of describing Christian realities in any philosophical parlance however transformed.

Unsurprisingly, in the response of 23.2, Thomas couches the rest of his claims regarding charity in terms of motion. He argues with Lombard's invocation (*"this movement is from the Holy Spirit without any intermediary habit"*). He qualifies how motion ought to be invoked (*"but if we consider the matter aright, which would be, on the contrary, detrimental to charity. For when the Holy Spirit moves the human mind the movement of charity does not proceed from this motion in such a way that the human mind be merely moved, without being the principle of this movement"* and *"neither can it be said that the Holy Spirit moves the will to the act of loving as though the will*

---

22. On ST 1-2.69, see pages 29–30.

were an instrument"). He couples motion and causation (*"given that the will is moved by the Holy Spirit to the act of love, it is necessary that the will also should be the efficient cause of that act"*). And he concludes with allusions to previous configurations (*"God, who moves all things to their due ends, bestowed on each thing the form whereby it is inclined to the end appointed to it by Him . . . Therefore it is most necessary that, for us to perform the act of charity, there should be in us some habitual form superadded to the natural power, inclining that power to the act of charity"*). The language of causation is present, though subordinate to the governing motion vocabulary. Of the two times it appears, both are from passages cited in the context of Thomas' emphasis on motion.[23]

Three insights on divine-human agency come into view: first, the inward movement of the Holy Spirit through Its non-violent, enabling, and perfecting activity enables the will to actuate its own effectiveness; second, in accordance with being moved by God to its due end, the form of charity is superadded to the natural power inclining it to act with ease and pleasure; and third, this movement of the Holy Spirit is expressive of the perfection of friendship with God.[24] In describing how charity enacts this movement, Thomas also calls charity an efficient cause giving the form to all other acts of virtue. Charity informs acts, causing them to be meritorious as the principle of motion toward God. This is Thomas' way of describing how charity moves the acquired virtues to the ultimate end and moves the infused virtues to delight and joy. Charity's movement is a perfecting movement, enabling the other virtues to enact perfection not possible before.

Thus Thomas shows God's perfection of the imperfect creature in the questions on charity. Thomas' complex account of agency reminds readers of the primacy of God's activity in creatures' return. The accomplishments of charity are God's. The relationship between the perfect exemplar and imperfect likeness is most determinatively shaped by God's perfect movement. This special movement of God for creatures is grace. This movement is a non-violent work *with us* that enables us for the movement that is virtue's perfect and perfecting activity.

---

23. In a careful reading of Thomas' corpus, Sherwin covers Thomas' shifts in describing the type of causality exercised by the intellect and will. He also notes the continuities in Thomas' early and later works in describing charity's action in terms of motion and perfection; by contrast Thomas changes his way of describing charity's causal action upon the virtues. Sherwin, *By Knowledge and By Love*, 192–94.

24. Wadell, *Friends of God*, 23.

Without charity, no true virtue is possible. Thomas explains this claim by invoking a threefold distinction between virtues: counterfeit, imperfect, and true virtue.[25] Virtue is "counterfeit" if a particular good is merely apparent. Virtue is "imperfect" if a particular good is true but limited, even as it remains open to "further reference to the final and perfect good." And virtue is "true" if the particular good is truly good and by its nature capable of being directed to the principal good which is the ultimate end.

Setting the claims in ST 2-2.23.7 alongside the distinctions "perfect" and "imperfect" from ST 1-2.65, the "virtues" that are infused, perfect, and virtue *simpliciter* are distinguished from the "virtues" that are acquired, imperfect, virtue *secundum quid*. They are analogically related, with infused virtues coming closer to the meaning of "virtue."

An apparent problem arises in Question 65 when Thomas recalls Augustine's strict condemnation of the activity of *infideles*, whose virtue is "false":

> The other virtues, i.e., the acquired virtues, are virtues in a certain respect [*secundum quid*] and not virtues absolutely speaking, since they order a human in the right way with respect to the ultimate end in a certain genus, but not with respect to the ultimate end absolutely speaking. Hence Augustine's gloss on Romans 14:23, *All that is not of faith is sin* says, *Where cognition of the truth is lacking, there is false virtue [falsa est virtus] even in good behavior.* (ST 1-2.65.2)

Is Thomas espousing a dichotomy between true and false virtue? Thomas makes his case more complex than contrary oppositions. In this question on charity he deploys a threefold distinction of virtue, two of which may correspond to *infideles*—counterfeit or imperfect. If the act of the *infidelis* is in accordance with a lack of charity, the act is sinful. This uncharitable act renders their virtue counterfeit. If, however, the act is referable to some other gift of God, there can be an act which is good of its kind though not fully good. (This would be the case of one who is without charity, but who acts in accordance with one's natural good.) This act simply without reference to charity renders their virtue imperfect. Thomas offers two possible characterizations of the virtue of *infideles*. Here Thomas makes clear how apparent tensions between acquired and infused virtue or false and true virtue can be reconfigured through the threefold distinction. Thus Thomas

---

25. ST 2-2.23.7: *falsa similitudo virtutis, imperfecta, et virtus vera (simpliciter)*.

actually qualifies his view of *infideles* as he binds charity to the perfection of virtue.

In view of the perfection of virtue, the charity of a wayfarer can always increase (ST 2-2.24.4). Thomas explains this in view of the dominant metaphor of the moral life—the journey of the soul to God. Charity should increase because the Christian is a *viator* who advances spiritually toward God through "steps of love," as St. Gregory says. Thomas writes,

> Grace perfects and inclines to good according to the manner of nature. It follows that those who are in the state of grace ought so much the more to grow in charity as they draw near their last end (and are more attracted by it). This is why St. Paul says here: "Not forsaking our assembly . . . but comforting one another, and so much the more as you see the day approaching," that is, the end of the journey. "The night is past, and the day is at hand" (Romans 13:12). "But the path of the just, as a shining light, goeth forward and increaseth even to perfect day" (Proverbs 4:18).[26]

This passage is all the more striking for Thomas' observations before the discovery of the law of universal gravitation. Garrigou-Lagrange glosses Thomas' passage: "Thomas means that in the saints the spiritual life is more and more intensified; the movement of their souls rises to the zenith and no longer descends. For them, there is no twilight."[27]

This increase looks something like what we would recognize as *intensity* (ST 1-2.66.1). The inexhaustible potentiality for charity's increase is crucial, otherwise all advance along the way would cease. Progress toward perfection is always possible because it is always possible to increase in charity. Thomas writes that charity in the wayfarer is perfect when

1. the whole heart is always actually borne towards God;
2. one makes an earnest endeavor to give all one's time to God; and
3. one gives one's whole heart to God habitually (ST 2-2.24.8).

The latter case, (3), is a kind of perfection common to all who have charity; the middle case, (2), a possible perfection for some wayfarers; and the first, (1), a perfection not possible in this life. The next article describes these

---

26. Thomas Aquinas, *Commentary on the Epistle to the Hebrews*, 10-2 [513], quoted in Garrigou-Lagrange, *Three Ages of the Interior Life*, 131.

27. Garrigou-Lagrange, *Three Ages of the Interior Life*, 131–32.

degrees of perfection as "beginning" (*incipientes*), "progressing" (*proficientes*), and "perfect" (*perfectos*) (ST 2-2.24.9).

One might even suggest that in these questions on charity Thomas locates a *new* context for applying the relative distinction of "perfect" and "imperfect." The context concerns our supernatural beatitude. "Perfect" charity would to refer to "progressing" charity by which one makes an earnest endeavor to give all one's time to God, and "imperfect" charity to "beginning" charity when one gives one's whole heart to God habitually. This new layering of perfect and imperfect goes one step further than Question 62 (Section 2.3) by developing the ways in which we progress in supernatural beatitude.

Thomas makes evident his concern for the wayfarer's increase in charity as friendship with God. This new range illustrates how charity is simultaneously the beginning, the way, and the end of our perfection. The stages of perfection mark the gradual, greater participation in the Triune life made possible by this great gift. The assimilation to God named by charity always has room for increase as inferior analogues come to resemble more closely the exemplar virtues, i.e., the divine virtues of Christ Himself.

§3 The "Infused" Acquired Virtues

Having treated supernatural beatitude, this section turns to natural beatitude. Supernatural and natural beatitude together—the *duplex hominis beatitudo*—name how the entire human person is perfected by God on our journey back to God. The virtues required to obtain our natural beatitude are the acquired virtues. The acquired virtues are perfected in charity. Through charity, the acquired virtues order the wayfarer toward God. Thus charity's influence on the acquired virtues suggests a surprisingly *theological* rendering of acquired virtue.

This, too, is confirmed by the prior understanding of "virtue" as an analogical term, again recalling chapter 2. In that chapter the different meanings of "virtue" entail certain similarities between *all* "virtue" simply by sharing in the same reality—whether God's or ours, whether ours by a gift or ours by natural effort. Along with the basic cast of "virtue" as a theological analogical term is charity's influence over the acquired virtues. Together they yield this unexpected result: that the acquired virtues are more akin to the infused virtues than one might initially think. In this section, I write about what I call the "infused" acquired virtues.

As Thomas is first writing about human virtue in the *Summa*, treating it as a habit with different kinds, he turns from the distinction between the moral and theological virtues to the more fruitful distinction between the acquired and infused virtues. As he makes these distinctions, Thomas does more than search for a basic definition of virtue that would admit virtues whose causes are different as is the case with infused and acquired virtues—or for that matter admit virtues whose objects are different as is the case with moral and theological virtues. Thomas remains faithful to his understanding that "virtue" is predicated *per prius* of God. All other meanings of virtue—whether infused or acquired—are predicated *posterius* of us. The meaning of the analogical term "virtue" includes among its secondary meanings the infused and acquired virtues. All "virtue," whatever its object and however it is caused, has its meaning in God. Whenever and wherever "virtue" is predicated of creatures, that perfection refers back to God.

Even so, it may give the impression that the acquired virtues are far removed from our perfection. In the order of analogates—from God to infused to acquired—acquired virtues are secondary "virtues" secondarily. In the absence of faith, hope, and charity, one may even despair of acquired virtues. Indeed, Thomas gives ample evidence that the acquired virtues without charity will not lead us to our final end. Thomas explains:

> Just as the *end* is twofold, (i) the last end, and (ii) the proximate end, so also, is *good* twofold, (i), the ultimate and universal good, (ii) the other proximate and particular. The ultimate and principal good of the human, (i) is the enjoyment of God, according to Psalm 72:28: "It is good for me to adhere to God," and to this good the human is ordered by charity. The human's secondary and, as it were, particular good (ii) may be twofold: (iia) one is truly good, because, considered in itself, it can be directed to the principal good, which is the last end; (iib) while the other is good apparently and not truly, because it leads us away from the final good. (ST 2-2.23.7)

As he continues, he reaffirms that an act in accordance with the human's natural good yet without charity is "not perfectly good, because it lacks due order to the last end" (ST 2-2.23.7.ad1).[28]

The advent of charity, however, signals the rehabilitation of acquired virtue. Thomas concludes with a hint of how charity may influence the

---

28. Elsewhere he emphasizes that the goodness of acquired virtue is not completely taken away by sin, but such acts are not meritorious in ST 1-2.85.2, 4 and 2-2.10.4.

acquired virtues: "If this particular good be a true good, for instance the welfare of the state, or the like, it will indeed be a true virtue, imperfect, however, *unless it be referred to the final and perfect good*" (ST 2-2.23.7). Thomas implies his application of his flexible distinction of "imperfect" and "perfect" to acquired virtue. Acquired virtue is "imperfect" if it is ordered to a true but limited good and "perfect" if it is referred to the final and perfect good. The move from "imperfect" to "perfect" acquired virtue is possible through charity.

Retracing our steps, Thomas' account of acquired virtue adds to the account of natural beatitude laid out in Question 62 (chapter 1 §4); Question 62 augmented the account of beatitude in this life laid out in Question 5, and Question 5 added to the account of human beatitude laid out in Questions 1–3 (chapter 1 §3). In Question 23, the key for developing the acquired virtues is charity. The presence of charity determines the form of the acquired virtues.

Chart 4: "Virtue" as an Analogical Term"

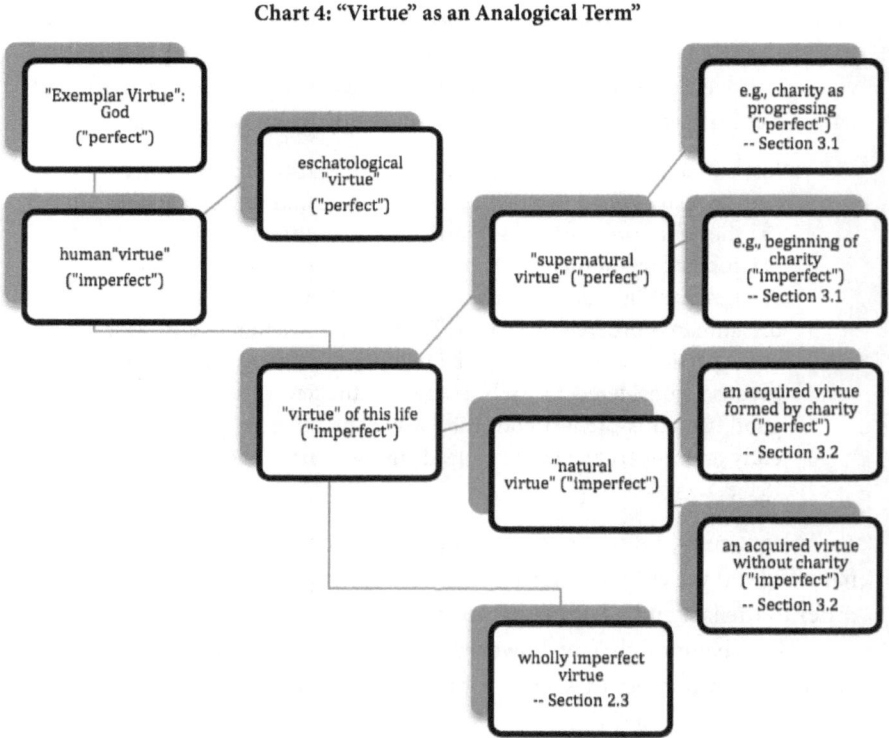

A traditionally important passage in the so-called "Treatise on Grace" amplifies these observations. In Question 109, Article 2 Thomas claims that in our present state, the human "needs a gratuitous strength superadded to natural strength" for two reasons—"in order to be healed, and furthermore in order to carry out works of supernatural virtue, which are meritorious... The human needs the Divine help, that he may be moved to act well."[29] God's grace given in charity is similar to "the help of medicine," which restores a sick man to health so he can be "perfectly moved."[30] Recall how Langland allegorizes the traditional theme of the wound of sin and Charity's cure in *Piers'* episode on *semyuief* and the Good Samaritan (chapter 3). Sin incapacitates *semyuief*, leaving him half-dead by the wayside. He may only move again with divine help. God-given grace is administered by a figure called the Samaritan, which is bound up with Charity.

Thomas maintains that our naming the acquired virtues is generated from a theological framework of analogical predications. He also holds that they are shaped by charity. Moreover, their *theological* character is evident in his claims that they rely on God. He asserts that the acquired virtues are "not without divine assistance" (ST 1-2.62.1). They are "not without God" (*De veritate* 24.14). Because humanity is fallen, he "needs divine help, that he may be moved to act well" (ST 1-2.109.2).

Acquired virtues are so tethered to God, in fact, that Thomas treats them explicitly in terms of a "cooperation" in his early writing, *Scriptum super Sententiis*. John Inglis observes:

> Thomas argued that because human nature is received from God, activities that conform with nature represent cooperation with the divine. Since acquired moral virtue is produced according to the natural principles of virtue that have been received from God, the acquired virtues are exercised in cooperation with the highest good.[31]

The acquired virtues are one of two ways in which we participate in God: (1) according to nature, which is a cooperation and (2) according to supernatural grace, which is a gift. Rudi te Velde takes the theological character of acquired virtues even further by animating them through a single unifying principle: love. The "twofold divine love" that God has for us is (1)

---

29. ST 1-2.108.2.
30. Ibid.
31. Inglis, "Aquinas's Replication," 11. Inglis cites *Sent.* 3.33.1.2.2. et ad 1.

creative love according to nature and (2) elective love according to grace.³²
The acquired virtues are movements of love, whose direction is shaped by the creature's relationship with a loving and gratuitous Creator. In its fullness, this dual movement is of love *and* of charity. Te Velde's observations and the cooperative character of acquired virtue allow us to revisit the early definition of infused virtue as that "which God works in us without us." By now, the picture is fuller with the acquired virtues as *that which God works in us with us.*³³

In this section, I outline how Thomas charts the potential for acquired virtue to be included in a perfection that reaches beyond it. The same potential appears in a concise and astute judgment by Thomas Joseph White:

> Aquinas is quite adamant about the absence of a capacity in *fallen* human nature to love God above all things even *naturally*—in the absence of grace (ST 1-2.109.3). He also in various places minimizes the natural capacities of the intellect to contemplate God *in most men* in virtue of the consequences of sin, ignorance, and cultural limitations. Consequently, if the final natural end of the human (the imperfect beatitude of natural knowledge and love of God) is preserved in the economy of redemption, it is also in some real sense *restored* therein . . . *Existentially* even the natural order is only attainable in its relative integrity under and in grace. The unity of the two orders (of nature and grace) in the exercise of the economy suggests a unified destiny: the natural ordering of the person toward God cannot function rightly except within and by grace.³⁴

Acquired virtue reaches its own integrity in charity, allowing it to become what it fully is. Even as its ends remain natural and charity's supernatural, they mutually confirm the unity of the two orders of nature and grace in a unified destiny: God.

---

32. Velde, *Aquinas on God*, 152. Te Velde maintains the traditional Thomistic understanding of the correlative distinctions of nature/grace and natural/supernatural happiness.

33. In my treatment of charity earlier in this chapter, I touch upon what it means for Thomas to claim that an infused virtue is that *which God works in us without us*. At the same time, Thomas is also concerned that charity is ours—see especially page 87.

34. White, review of Feingold, 466.

5

Help and Obstacles Along the Way

FOR ALL OF THIS, we are fallen and wounded creatures. The lesson from the pivotal episode in *Piers Plowman*, Passus XIX centering on the Samaritan, is that any story of sin is also a story of our need for Christ. Going further, we cannot understand "virtue" without finally seeing ourselves as *semyuief*, wounded by sin (chapter 3). *We* are *semyuief*. The wounds of ignorance, malice, weakness, and intemperance mar our capacity for the moral virtues. Charity exceeds our grasp.

Yet we have help along the way: the sacraments. The sacraments are medicinal balm and wayfarers' food, as Langland and Thomas describe them. They heal our wounded nature as embodied helps given by Christ through the Church. They enliven their recipients' new and renewed capacity for growth in the virtues. As such, they are the means by which Christ's promises become actually incarnate. The sacraments are so essential to the way that wayfaring itself assumes a sacramental character. There is no progress along the way without the sacraments.

Although the well-worn path for the Christian life is available in and through the sacraments, what follows Will's encounter with the Samaritan is *not* the life of virtue as nurtured and sustained by the sacramental community. Instead the poem turns to what happens when the Samaritan leaves: "'I may stay no longer,' [the Samaritan] said, and spurred his mount / And went away like the wind, and with that I awoke" (XIX.330–31). In Will's waking, it seems that he is forced backward into his old habits. Will returns to his habitual resistance. Will wanders again, astray in the wild wilderness. He must learn, relearn, and re-relearn the way. He is "lost, found, and lost again and again."[1] Thus Langland amplifies the sense in which sin alienates and continues to alienate wanderers from their true orientation toward Christ, communicated in the sacraments. For Will and all other wanderers who remain possessed by sin's habits, Langland illustrates the moral consequences that result. For a community that refuses Charity's call, its members effectively shut themselves off from the sources of grace offered for their sustenance. Without this sustenance, the virtues are askew. The intended happy bond between the sacraments and virtues meets profound disintegration in its ecclesial and social dimensions.

This final chapter focuses on sacraments and sin in the closing passus of *Piers*, reflected in the title, "Help and Obstacles Along the Way." Indeed Thomas and Langland share the christological-sacramental horizon in which the virtues find their source and sustenance. But Langland serves as an especially helpful guide for this aspect of the journey because he discloses the great promise of Christ's gifts in the sacraments alongside the continued power of our habits of sin. He illustrates sin's havoc on sacramental practice itself, sin's havoc on virtue, and sin's havoc on relationships within the Church and polity. This dark reality is the result of sin having more sway in us than sacraments. His meditations on the powerful habits of sin are essential to see the virtues and the way in their wonderful complexity. Ultimately, this chapter shows the limits of virtue.

As the poem courses on in Passus XXI–XXII, the ravages of sin are ubiquitous. The concluding events include the allegorical building of the Church: Grace gives Piers the plowman a team of four great oxen (Matthew, Mark, Luke, and John), four horses (Augustine, Ambrose, Gregory, and Jerome), seeds (the cardinal virtues) to be harrowed with the Old and New law, a cart (Christendom), workhorses (Contrition and Confession), and the house Unity (Holy Church). Yet not all is as it should be. The virtues themselves assume curious forms and signal a malaise that appears elusive until a pivotal assault by Pride. Pride threatens Conscience and Christians that they have to part with the seeds (the cardinal virtues). Common Sense responds by digging a deep ditch around Unity. Soon the people balk at Conscience's invitation to Eucharist because it is conditional upon *redde quod debes*. They willfully reject the cardinal virtues and the practices of forgiveness and restitution that would cultivate them. The bonds of unity disintegrate. Will is commanded to remain in the Church while Conscience becomes a pilgrim searching for grace. In sum, I rehearse the activity of

---

1. Aers, *Salvation and Sin*, 97.

these concluding passus through the founding of the Church and Grace's pouring out of the virtues (§1), sin besieging a community and agents rejecting the gifts offered them (§2), and the Church accommodating Herself with the communal effects of this accommodation (§3).

Corresponding to these sections, I focus on three aspects of Langland's treatment of virtues, sacraments, and sin. In §1, I turn to Langland's depiction of the cardinal virtues given by Grace—what Thomas calls infused moral virtues. Langland casts these virtues as failures, resemblances, admixtures, with at times hints of perfection. In sum, Langland depicts at least four "degrees" of one kind of virtue—and given Langland's extraordinary imagination, readers suppose he is not limited to these. These diverse manifestations illustrate the power of sin to undermine, threaten, and challenge the infused virtues.

In §2, I take up Langland's depiction of the extraordinary range of the people's collective failure to embrace the virtues. Langland is concerned that individuals are so habituated to vice that, when confronted with the stringent moral demands of the sacraments, they willingly say "no." They reject the sacraments because they reject the requirements of the Christian life—returning what we owe to others (justice's *redde quod debes*), forgiveness and kindness (charity). "Come again?" the common people retort, "You counsel us to give back / All that we owe anybody before going to communion?" (XXI.391–92). These four individuals—the brewer, the uneducated vicar, the lord, and the king, with correspondingly diverse impulses—are more than themselves as stand-ins for an entire group. Their reactions range widely, from explicit rejection of the cardinal virtues given by Grace to an embrace of perverted forms of virtues. Their defiant resistance to grace portends an unraveling of the entire social and ecclesial order.

In §3, I conclude with Langland's account of this very unraveling as the Church accommodates its sacramental practice and loosens its moral strictures to become more palatable to the people. The genesis of this corruption begins with the hold of sin on the brewer, vicar, lord, and king, then leads to piecemeal and soon whole-scale compromise, and finally entails destruction of social and ecclesial communities. These last passus of *Piers* disclose the darkest of prospects for those who sever themselves from the fullness of Christ and his sacraments while reaffirming Langland's earlier work on the thoroughgoing christological cast of the virtues.

Langland has the last word in this chapter. In my Introduction, I suggested that Langland's poetry can take Thomas' tradition of virtues further.

Langland does so in Passus XXI–XXII by tending to the diverse ways in which sin poses manifest obstacles to the virtues—in realms existential, individual, social, political, and ecclesial.

§1 Grace Gave the Cardinal Virtues

Recall that the Samaritan's gifts and the graced community founded upon those gifts are revealed in their fullness in the mid-Lent episode in Passus XIX. Passus XX is set in Holy Week, beginning with "One who resembled the Samaritan and Piers the plowman somewhat" (XX.7), announced by Faith as "A, *filii* Dauid!" (XX.13). Passus XX centers on Will's climactic antepenultimate vision of Christ's Passion and Crucifixion and his triumphant Harrowing of Hell, the beginning of Love's victory over evil. It ends with the pealing of the bells in Easter joy. Finally Passus XXI is connected with the liturgical season of Pentecost, taking up a second founding of the Church and penitential practice. This second time the work is done by the risen Christ, for the Church continues the work begun by Christ of redeeming the world.[2]

The Church is comprised of a repentant and repenting people.[3] Forgiveness is the ecclesial practice captured at the heart of a refrain throughout the poem, *redde quod debes*, whose meaning has been unclear up to this point. According to the tradition Langland inherits, "returning what you owe" in the sense of repentance is a part of justice.[4] Agents become just, in part, by acknowledging their lack of perfection. This lack implies a debt of transgression and a need to "return what you owe." Confession, forgiveness, and reconciliation are linked to the theological virtues that accompany them—all of which are learned in virtuous relationships with virtuous others in a virtuous community—all of which depend on grace.[5]

---

2. Smith makes this connection through the Gospel on the twelfth Sunday after Pentecost (Luke 10:35) regarding the second coming of Christ in Judgment. The traditional associations of the parable of the Good Samaritan (XIX) with the second coming (XXI) indicate that Christ's work is not yet done (begun in XX) and that it is the responsibility of the church and her priests to continue the work of Christ. Smith, *Traditional Imagery of Charity*, 92.

3. Augustine offers a hallmark description of such a community in *City of God against the Pagans*, XIX.27.

4. See ST 2-2.57-122, 3.85 and Aers, "Justice and Wage-Labor after the Black Death." Aers draws on Thomas' *De Regimine*.

5. ST 3.85.6. Augustine, a consummate theologian of grace, explains the need for the

As forgiveness and mercy are themselves conditional upon *redde,* the community is deeply dependent on Christ. Only Christ's own strenuous activity on our behalf will effect merciful pardon.[6] Only Christ's deed can link pardon, forgiveness, and the cardinal virtue of justice. The failures previously in the poem, such as Passus V–VIII where a community struggles to forgive and provide restitution, are explained by the absence of Christ. These earlier passus depict a Christian culture at times willingly cut off from its own source of life.

In XXI, Christ is with his community through the Holy Spirit poured out at Pentecost. Will narrates this pouring out: "and then came, it seemed to me, / One *Spiritus paraclitus* to Piers and his followers. / In likeness of lightning it alighted on them all / And made them understand and know all kinds of languages" (XXI.200–203). By sharing posture, song, and prayer, they participate in "an event from another place and time which is being remembered, believed, re-enacted, continued, and to some extent understood and 'seen' within one's own place and time."[7] Remembering, believing, re-enactment, and continuation are the extension of and kinship from the person of Christ to the community. The extent to which this community becomes the one Christ intends is the extent to which they conform to the demands of *redde*.

Yet Langland shifts his mode of figurative expression from Passus XIX to XXI. In XIX, the descriptions are concrete insofar as the virtues themselves are personified in Faith, Hope, and Charity. In the founding of the Church in XXI, however, the newly introduced realities finally possible in a post-Pentecost age are abstract. For example, the practices of the community are spiritualized in the name of loyalty and love (XXI.232, 237,

---

mercy of God to lead us to repentance: "Therefore God's mercy is needed not only while penance is being done, but also that it may be done" (*Enchiridion* XXII.82, citing 2 Tim 2:25).

6. ST 3.1.2. Thomas treats Christ's Incarnation as fitting of repayment or satisfaction. F. C. Bauerschmidt notes of ST 3.1.a.ad2, "In speaking of merit, Thomas distinguishes between a reward that one is owed in justice (meriting *de condigno*) and a reward that is fitting but not owed in justice (meriting *de congruo*). In this response, Thomas makes a similar distinction with regard to repayment—between one that is equivalent to what is owed (*condigna*) and one that is imperfect yet sufficient (*satisfactio sufficiens imperfecte*) because it is graciously accepted by the one to whom recompense is due. These two distinctions are related because on the Cross Christ merits *de condigno* because he makes equivalent repayment (*satisfactio condigno*)" (*Holy Teaching*, 170 n. 19).

7. Davlin, *Place of God*, 15–16. Davlin cites Duffy, *Stripping of the Altars*: liturgical "ceremonies were designed to summon up the scenes they commemorated" (20).

250).⁸ Although Piers is now establishing the visible Church in the world, in a stark contrast to the failed attempts in Passus VII–VIII, the imagery associated with the Church is now subsumed into an inner domain. Here the virtues are "seeds" that are sown in the human soul. This new abstracted allegorical mode of XXI invites a worrisome rewriting of the community, its constitutive practices, and its virtues so recently wrought in XIX. Accordingly, Langland's reintroduction of the virtues in XXI extends rather than resolves previous difficulties.

This great evangelical allegory unfolds with wonderful and telling agricultural imagery.

> Grace gave Piers a team, four great oxen;
> The first was Luke, a large humble-looking beast,
> And Mark, and Matthew the third, both mighty animals,
> And yoked them with one John, most noble of all,
> The blue-ribbon ox of Piers' plow, surpassing all others.
>   And then Grace of his goodness gave Piers four horses,
> To harrow afterward all that his oxen plowed.
> One was called Augustine and Ambrose another,
> Gregory the great clerk and Jerome the good.
> These four followed Piers' team to teach the faith
> And in no time harrowed all Holy Scripture
> With two spiked harrows they had, an old and a new,
>   *That is, the old testament and the new.*
>   And Grace gave Piers seeds, the cardinal virtues,
> And he sowed them in man's soul, and then told their names.
> (XXI.262–75)

This moment discloses the activity of the great gift of divine grace in the Gospels, the church fathers, "all Holy Scripture," and finally the "cardinal virtues"—*Spiritus prudencie, Spiritus temperancie, Spiritus fortitudinis,* and *Spiritus iusticie* (XXI.274, 276, 281, 289, 298).

Initially these virtues *seem* promising as this is the first time that "cardinal" is reconciled to "virtue" in the poem, a relationship that has been estranged since the Prologue. This reconciliation marks a new moment not previously possible in the poem. In XXI, the action of the poem brings

---

8. This might recall Conscience, Reason, and the King's abstract ideals invoked against Meed in Passus IV (here treated in 1.2). These abstractions avoid the difficult questions that Langland has raised up to this point as a utopian corrective to Passus II–IV. On the multiplicity of modes of allegory, especially with respect to the agricultural imagery now realigned through Christ, see Aers, *Piers Plowman and Christian Allegory,* 71–131, esp. 129–30.

together law and grace in the context of loving community. The "cardinal virtues" appear in a form of life that is thoroughly ecclesial and rooted in Scripture. This new reality is connected to the narratives of the life, death, and Resurrection of Christ, and has as its bookends treatments of Grace and the Old and New Law. Langland glosses the cardinal virtues: "These four seeds Piers sowed and afterwards harrowed them / With Old Law and New Law so that love might grow / Among these four virtues and destroy vices" (XXI.310–12). The law of love first displayed with the Samaritan in XIX has become a real *potential* for those in whom Grace works. This work of Grace *may* issue forth the virtues "that love *might* grow." The "cardinal virtues" *may* finally be connected to love.[9]

Are the cardinal virtues as eschatologically fulfilled promises available to us now? Do they signal the "great renewal and return to the pristine status of apostolic purity"?[10] This reconciliation of cardinals and virtue, wrought by the work of Christ, does *not* issue in works of perfection. Rather, the virtues that appear are curious:

> *Spiritus prudencie* the first seed was called,
> Which whoever ate, he would have foresight,
> Before he did any deed devise the end well;
> And it taught men to buy a long-handled ladle
> Who mean to stir a crock and save the fat on top. (XXI.276–80)

Spiritus prudencie has little to do with Christ. It has little to do with deciding "in what manner and by what means" one shall obtain the rule of charity in one's deeds in light of one's "perfect" eschatological beatitude (ST 2-2.47.7). It does have to do with "foresight" to "devise the end well"—this seems right. However a serious problem emerges as Langland describes its activities. It teaches people "to buy a long-handled ladle / Who mean to stir a crock and save the fat on top." Rather than directing matters concerning salvation, it guides one through the excessively mundane. This shocking portrait is arguably Langland's attempt to cause the reader to question whether attaining such an end merits the term "virtue."

Spiritus temperancie too appears equally questionable, though it improves the more its characteristic activities unfold.

---

9. Morton Bloomfield regards Langland's emphasis on the cardinal virtues as "puzzling" in light of his apocalyptic reading of the poem. See *Piers Plowman as a Fourteenth-Century Apocalypse*, 134.

10. Ibid., 121.

> The second seed was called *Spiritus temperancie*;
> He that ate of that seed had such a nature,
> Never would food or misfortune make him swell up,
> Nor should any heckler make him lose his balance;
>   Nor ever winning wealth of worldly riches,
> Waste words of idleness or wicked speech move.
> No finely fitted clothes fell on his back
> Nor into his mouth dinner dished up by a master chef.
> (XXI.281–88)

Spiritus temperancie appears like the problematic *Spiritus prudencie* insofar as through it, neither food nor misfortune would make a person swell up, nor would a heckler make one lose his balance. These seem like trivial effects. Fortunately, *Spiritus temperancie* includes more—spurning worldly riches, watching one's tongue, dressing modestly, and eating humbly. These appear more characteristic activities of perfection, though they depend on a worldly end.

Spiritus fortitudinis comes third:

> The third seed that Piers sowed was *Spiritus fortitudinis*
> And whoever ate of that seed was hardy forever
> To suffer all that God sent, sickness, and troubles.
> There may no liar's lying or loss of property
> Make him, for any mourning, lose his cheerful outlook
> And his bold and abiding ability to endure slanders;
> And he pleaded all with patience and *Parce michi, domine*,
> And took cover under counsel of Cato the wise:
> *Be strong of spirit when condemned unjustly.* (XXI.289–97)

This third "cardinal virtue," *Spiritus fortitudinis*, expresses an integral relationship to God. Indeed Langland weaves Job and conventional Greek wisdom into this expression of fortitude. The scriptural passage is Job 7:16: "I have done with hope. I shall now live no longer. Spare me, for my days are nothing." Langland's echo of Job is based on a hierarchy of goods to explain fortitude, quite similar to Gregory's *Morals on the Book of Job*. Yet Gregory connects this impulse to pardon in a way that Langland may have been interested to include, writing,

> For neither do the two words agree together, "I have given over hope" and "spare me." For he that "gives over hope" no longer begs to be spared; and he who is anxious to be spared, is surely far from "giving over hope." It is on one sort of grounds then that he "gives over hope" and on another that the holy man prays to be spared;

in the whilst he abandons the good things of the transitory life in "giving over the hope" thereof, he rises more vigorous in hope for the securing of those that shall endure. So that in "giving over hope" he is the more effectually brought to the hope of pardon, who seeks the things so much more determinatively, in proportion as he more thoroughly forsakes those of the present time in giving up hope.[11]

As much as *Spiritus fortitudinis* concerns both the life of this world and the next, there is something still lacking. Langland's use of Job is revealing—*Spiritus fortitudinis* lacks Christ. This sequence is analogous to Langland's episode earlier in the poem when Will is led to Faith and Hope, who are still lost without Charity (XVIII.179–XIX.93; recall chapter 1, section 3).

At this point in the poem, Christ's absence seems to be underscored through this systemic lack of reference to Him. After the Samaritan and narratives of Christ's life, there are few traces of his presence. We see traces of this absence again in the fourth and final virtue: justice.

> The fourth seed that Piers sowed was *Spiritus iusticie*,
> And he that ate of that seed should be squarely true
> With God, and afraid of nothing but of guile only
> (For guile goes so secretly that sometimes good faith
> Cannot be detected through *Spiritus iusticie*).
> *Spiritus iusticie* spares no punishment for the guilty
> And to correct the king, if the king's a guilty party.
> For he takes account of no king's wrath when he sits in court,
> To make judgments like a judge; he was never afraid
> Neither of duke nor of death that he wouldn't distribute justice,
> Despite presents or prayers or any prince's letters;
> He did equity to all to the best of his ability. (XXI.298–309)

Spiritus iusticie is pit against guile, the king, figures in power and authority, death, and versions of meed. It sets one at odds with dominant sociopolitical arrangements. It is "squarely true with God," an ally to truth. *Spiritus iusticie* is even more determinative for action than human law. Only as *iusticie* abides in love—the law of love—does it conform to and complement a version of law that exceeds the law of kings and courts (XXI.310–11). Is this justice something new—a grace-filled justice shaped by Christ?[12]

11. Gregory, *Morals on the Book of Job*, 1-2: Book 8.27.46.

12. Contrast the uses of the word thus far, *iustice*, and its variants which only appear in Passus XX–XXII as referring to judge or justices (Russell-Kane, XX.37, XXI.139,

Suspending that question for a moment, I rehearse the developments in XXI. This deep picture of the "cardinal virtues" sown by Grace extends the range of "infused virtue" in giving four rather different forms. Redescribing Langland's sequence of four according to the Thomistic lexicon, one might say that Langland moves from a version of infused moral virtue that fails to express its orientation toward a supernatural end (*Spiritus prudencie*) to infused moral virtue that resembles acquired virtue and may even be directed implicitly toward a supernatural end (*Spiritus temperancie*) to an admixture of acquired virtue and infused virtue that is fully neither (*Spiritus fortitudinis*) to infused virtue that approximates its ideal form, though questions linger (*Spiritus iusticie*).[13]

Such diversity in the infused virtues may be explained by the influence of acquired vice and sin. Langland might be understood to illustrate how acquired vice compromises infused virtue and how sin poses a stumbling block for the infused virtues to become that which they are intended to be. Langland's ordering of lesser to greater might work pedagogically in moving from the most devastating effects of vicious habits to their remedy in charity. Were this the case, Langland rehearses the familiar move from false to imperfect to perfect.

While Thomas brings out the "incompletion" characteristic of infused virtues—incomplete in that they lack the *delectatio* that defines the acquired virtues—Langland brings out other ways in which the infused virtues may be "incomplete."[14] Langland's varieties not only fit with the thesis that the infused virtues may appear "imperfect," but Langland might be used to develop the idea that they may also appear "false" according to

---

XXII.134). This form of justice is made possible by the Samaritan—and hence charity—who precedes it. And it is an integral virtue for being and building the community which Christ establishes, overseen by Piers, and supported by the sacraments. Readers can expect that from here on out, whatever its failings, the faithful church community depends on the practices of *redde*. (One might carry through along these same lines by investigating the poet's use of the Middle English charite versus Latin's *caritas*.) That justice enjoys this particular form should strain against the semi-Pelagian readings offered by Bloomfield and others, which would assume the possibility of this virtue apart from its "particularly or uniquely Christian" aspects. Bloomfield, *Piers Plowman*, 134.

13. One ought take great care in reading the poem through the lens of the *Summa*, yet the opportunity here seemed too great to pass. Tending to the careful construal of agency throughout the poem, especially here with Grace giving the cardinal virtues, Langland comes close to a Thomistic rendering of the infused moral virtues that puts some distance from the dominant alternative: Scotus. Scotus decided to forego the infused moral virtues in favor of charity's influence over the (merely) acquired moral virtues.

14. See Thomas' treatment in chapter 3, section 2.

Thomas (in *Spiritus prudencie*). At the most basic level, a "false" infused virtue is "infused" insofar as it comes from God but "false" insofar as it fails to evidence its supernatural orientation, though this idea would need some Thomistic gymnastics to give it a full rendering.[15] Langland shows how the infused virtues may be hindered from their perfection, implying the continued power of sin even for those who receive grace. Sin does not go away easily in Langland. Indeed it strikes with a new vengeance in the next narrative sequence.

Meanwhile, the agricultural imagery Langland uses to frame his introduction of these four new cardinal virtues could itself signal difficulties ahead. In the first passus of *Piers*, Langland plays on the language of the cardinal virtues and *cardo* ("hinge") as these virtues are the hinges on which the gates of heaven open and close.[16] In XXI, Langland rewrites them as "seeds," a revision rooted in the tradition in which Thomas also stands. In fact, Thomas uses the same language to describe the relation of nature to the development of virtue: *seminalia virtutum* (ST 1-2.63.1). For Thomas, these virtues of intellect are natural by way of a beginning (*secundum quandam inchoationem*) and must be brought to completion (*consummatio*).[17] "Seeds" are a mere beginning for both Thomas and Langland. Yet both insist on the ultimate shortcoming of such a model for the whole of the moral life. For Thomas illustrates the limits of *seminalia virtutum* by introducing their counterparts of the infused cardinal virtues later in the same question (ST 1-2.63.3). And Langland's spiritualized interiorization of the virtues strains against their concrete, communal character. The placement of the material on "seeds" in each text is instructive—Thomas clarifies it as a nascent habit and Langland registers an alteration of the definitive preceding episode that identifies Christ, Charity, and the Church. No wonder the "Spirited" virtues instead appear to be seeds of trouble.

---

15. Consider what it would be for a virtue to indeed be a gift from God, but to never become embedded in the cognitive powers and appetites and therefore never confer real facility. For an account of the virtues and human affectivity, see Lombardo, *Logic of Desire*, 133–34.

16. Recall chapter 1, page 48.

17. Thomas concerns himself with the apprehensive powers, whereas Langland is focused on the appetitive.

§2 Come Again?

What happens next provides crucial formation for this newly founded apostolic Church. As soon as Piers is to the plow, Pride threatens him. Pride means to "injure / Conscience and all Christians and the cardinal virtues, / blow them down and break them and bite in two their roots" (XXI.337–39).[18] Anarchy looms around the corner for the Church. This grim news for the Christian people is announced by Pride's henchmen, Sir Ego-trip and Kill-love (also known as Backbiter). They proclaim that the people will now "have to part with / The seeds that Sir Piers sowed, the cardinal virtues" (XXI.343–44). As a result, "Conscience will not know (by contrition or confession) who's Christian or heathen, / Nor any manner of merchant who deals with money / Whether he earns rightly, wrongly, or with usury" (XXI.349–51). *Spiritus iusticie* just sown seventy-three lines earlier is difficult to recognize again. The organic unity forged by Grace between labor and the just life—whatever that might have looked like—is severed (XXI.229–51). Will's own frustrations earlier in the poem now permeate this community, where the virtues are challenging to discover let alone embody. In sum, Pride and his collective forces re-create a culture that baffles the discernment essential to the practice of the Christian virtues and sacraments.[19]

Common Sense's [or Kynde Wit's] response to the attack of Pride seals the fate of the community. He convinces the Church besieged by sin to become the Church militant.

> And then [Kynde Wit] came to teach Conscience
> And cried and commanded all Christian people
> To dig a deep ditch around Unity
> So that Holy Church stood in holiness as if it were a fort.
> (XXI.361–64).

Whatever the potential or extant form of the community before, Kynde Wit intervenes, crying and commanding the people to dig a deep ditch. The defensive work of closing off the Church begins with the activity of exclusion. Piers' initial inclusion "to all manner of men" (XXI.184) now becomes a list of exceptions: "except for the streetwalkers . . . except for them—and . . ." (XXI.368–70). Those excluded in *Piers* are excluded on

---

18. This language also recalls the imagery from the Tree of Charity in XVIII.

19. See Aers, "Langland on the Church," 62, for more on the church's prohibition of usury and the importance of discernment to distinguish virtuous from sinful lending.

the basis of embodying personifications and types of *sinful* activity.[20] How, when, and what to do is dictated by the discursive reasoning of kynde wit, which is a genuine capacity with limits.[21]

Are Kynde Wit's claims faithful? Is the Church acting consistently with its mission? Does *Spiritus prudencie*, along with the other cardinal virtues, govern their activity? Are the cardinal virtues now those "on which the gate hinges / By which Christ in his kingdom closes off heaven" (Prologue, 132–33)?[22] The answer to all of these questions is a resounding "No."

These mistakes become apparent immediately because the threat to the Church is not merely from the outside—it is also from within. For Conscience invites the people to partake of the Eucharist, provided they *redde quod debes* in an act of justice and love. But the community members struggle with the penitential practice that was established so lately as integral for their communal identity, and they refuse to embody the virtues that were so recently sown in their souls.

> "Come," Conscience said, "you Christians, and eat,
> Who have labored loyally all this Lenten time.
> Here is a blessed bread and God's body there-under.
> Through God's word Grace gave Piers plowman power,
> Might to make it and men to partake of it
> In help of their health once a month
> Or as often as needed, those who had paid
> To Piers the plowman's pardon *Redde quod debes*."
> "Come again?" said the common people, "you counsel us to give back
> All that we owe anybody before going to communion?"
> "That's my advice," said Conscience, "and the cardinal virtues';
> Or each man forgive the other, as the *pater noster* asks,
> *And forgive us our debts.*
> And so to be absolved and afterwards take communion."
> (XXI.383–95)

Conscience invites those Christians who have "labored loyally all this Lenten time" to receive the Eucharist. "Loyal labor" is exactly that work

---

20. Davlin (*Place of God*, 133) notes that those excluded in *Piers* are not the typical "other" for thirteenth-century Europe: Jews, Saracens, heretics, ancient pagans, prostitutes, homosexuals, or souls of the damned.

21. See Imaginative and Christ's critiques in XIV.48–57 and XIX.108–12.

22. The C-version mentions closing, but not opening, the gates. Contrast the B-version: "closynge Yates / There Crist is in kyngdom, to close and to shette, / And to opene it to hem and hevene blisse shewe" (Prologue, 104–6).

of Grace—however abstract—detailed in XXI.229–51. Its continuance depends on resisting the undermining work of Pride in XXI.351. Nowhere does Langland suggest that these Christians have avoided sin. Even those called to the altar are in need of healing. Indeed the capacity strengthened by the virtues may deepen the wound of sin.

The imagery of Conscience's speech recollects this imagery as the Samaritan's speech on the sacraments and their healing power. The wound by sin of *semyuief*, a condition extended to all Christians, is made healthy again only with this blessed bread. Conscience imparts this pressing need for this healing by his encouragement of eucharist monthly, or "as often as needed."[23] The condition of receiving the sacrament of the altar is that one must fulfill the strict demands of *redde* or forgiveness of one another's debts. Penance becomes a mandate for the practices of Christian justice. This act of justice is both reunion and union. And it is mediated through the healing sacrament of charity.

Moreover the particular prominence of justice in the Christian life is underscored in Conscience's insistence that it is the "chief seed that Piers planted" (XXI.406). Individual salvation is bound up with a life that embodies justice, a life shared with others. The answer to Will's individualistic quest for salvation is finally social. All individuals need communities that enable and safeguard the virtues.

As inviting as this vision of social unity marked by the flourishing of the virtues is, it is demanding. And for many, it is too demanding.[24] Individuals from various walks of life—as various as the brewer, uneducated vicar, lord, and king—rebel. As soon as the Prologue–Passus IV are rewritten christologically (XVII–XXI), the individuals' collective rejection returns the reader's imagination to that corrupted, unchanged world. Deeply ensnared in sin, the agents are too tied to the practices of the market to see its effects. They revert to habits of resistance to grace. Conscience's literally gracious offering is met with rejection (XXI.396–476). By turns, all the "common people" turn the other way (XXI.391).[25]

---

23. This in itself is more frequent than medieval practice, in which the faithful received once a year. So again Langland (and Thomas) exceed late medieval norms. On these norms and their moral assumptions, see Duffy, *Stripping of the Altars*, 93–95.

24. Such a unity is inhospitable to the forms of unity forged through coercion. Compare Miri Rubin's account of the exploitation of *corpus Christi* and its accompanying discourse of unity and hierarchy in *Corpus Christi*, 270.

25. Even more encompassing is the original: "alle þe comune" (Russell-Kane, XXI.391). Mary Carruthers treats folk's rebellion in detail in *The Search for St. Truth*, 157–60.

The brewer first rejects *Spiritus iusticie*, preferring his practice of maximizing profits.

> "Oh yeah?" said a brewer, "I won't be ruled,
> By Jesus! Despite all your fast-talk, according to *Spiritus iusticie*
> Nor according to Conscience, by Christ, as long as I can sell
> Both dregs and swill and draw at one hole
> Thick or thin ale; that's the kind of guy I am
> And not to poke around for holiness—so just shut up, Conscience!
> Your *Spiritus iusticie* speech is a lot of hot air!" (XXI.396–402)

The brewer boasts an ontological claim regarding his own kind (kynde), "that's the kind of guy I am," willfully closed to the possibility of reform (XXI.400). "The will to silence Conscience seems to figure a will moving toward a fixed aversion from God and neighbor," writes Aers, and such a movement "is highlighted by the brewer's claim that his nature ('my kynde') is to pursue profits independently of the virtues and the quest for holiness."[26] His nature is fixed in a vicious second nature, with no role for virtuous habits such as *Spiritus iusticie*. Everything about the individualistic brewer is at odds with his being a part of the loving Christian community that habitually rejects covetousness and unkindness (XIX.250–73).

The uneducated vicar joins in:

> I'm a parson of Holy Church and never in my time came
> Any man to me who could tell me about cardinal virtues
> Or who counted Conscience worth chicken feathers.
> I never knew a cardinal who didn't come from the pope
> And when they come we clerics pick up the tab for their stay,
> For their furs and feed for their palfreys and plundering followers. (XXI.410–15)

The uneducated vicar discounts the cardinal virtues (and therefore Conscience) because their apparent namesake, cardinals, live in luxury and lechery (XXI.418). This description of the cardinals recalls the wordplay of the Prologue (134–35).

Here too in XXI, the cardinal virtues dissipate in the sin and hypocrisy of cardinals. The vicar cannot discern real virtue in practice, so he rejects *Spiritus prudencie* as a form of deceit that hides hypocrisy: "For *Spiritus prudencie* among the people is deceit / And all these fair virtues appear to them as vices. / For each man comes up with a sleight, to hide sin in, / And

---

26. Aers, "Langland on the Church," 64.

presents it as know-how and honest living" (XXI.455–58). The vicar exhibits the inability to discern the virtues—fulfilling the prophecy of Pride that his infiltration of the Church will systemically frustrate Christians' capacity to identify the virtues (XXI.343–51).

Then a lord jumps in to justify himself with a formidable tripartite invocation of right and reason, *Spiritus intellectus*, and *Spritius fortudinis*.

> Then a lord laughed there and "By these lights!" said,
> "I hold it as right and reasonable to take from my reeve
> All that my auditor or else my steward
> Advise me by their accounts and my clerk's records.
> With *Spiritus intellectus* they took the reeve's books
> And with *Spiritus fortitudinis* I'll fetch it, whether he likes it or not." (XXI.459–64)

The lord is describing his relationship with his reeve, or farm-manager, and "seems to take it for granted that the activity of a reeve will be characterized by deceit and self-seeking masquerading as prudence. He assigns the responsibility or checking the reeve's *rolles*, or statements of account, to his auditor and steward, who have the authority to enforce repayment from the reeve if the accounts are shown to be false."[27] The lord counters supports the intervention of *Spiritus intellectus*—presumably a substitution for the vicar's *Spiritus prudencie*—with a self-interested, distorted *Spiritus fortitudinis*. He will protect his own interests with coercion.

The fourth figure, the king, embraces the fourth cardinal virtue, *Spiritus iusticie*.

> I am crowned king to rule the commonwealth
> And to defend Holy Church and clergy from cursed men.
> And if my living has any lack, the law allows me to take it
> Where I may most readily get it, for I'm the law's head
> And you're only its limbs and I above all.
> And since I am head of you all I am health of you all
> And chief help of Holy Church and chieftain of the commons
> And whatever I take from you two I take it at the teaching
> Of *Spiritus iusticie*, for I judge you all.
> So I may take communion boldly for I never borrow
> Or crave from my commons except as my kind requires.
> (XXI.466–76)

---

27. Pearsall, note to XIX.459–64.

The king too systematically distorts the virtue by identifying his own actions as just ones. Every claim works against the spirit of *Spiritus iusticie* set out in XXI.298–309, which is pit against the king and dominant sociopolitical arrangements, which is "squarely true with God." Here he claims that he rightfully supplement his lavish living, he is above the common good, he is the chief help of Holy Church, he is judge over all, he may "take communion boldly for I never borrow / Or crave from my commons except as my kind requires."[28] The king iterates the brewer's disturbing conversion of his nature, indicating the unshakeable hold that these habits have on him. In the king's version of justice, the virtue encapsulated in the poem's refrain *redde quod debes*, it seems he owes no one anything.

To sum up, the hard-won reconciliation of cardinals and virtue yielding at last "cardinal virtue" linked to pardon, Eucharist, and reconciliatory social practice comes at too high a cost. The common people refuse to separate virtue from its worldly forms, balking at Conscience, "Come again?" Their refusal bespeaks their own distorted vision of the good. Substituting the power that Piers is given (XXI.183) for the power from the Prologue (135), they deform the virtues. Their rejection is a willful turning away from the good disclosed in the life of Christ, made real in Easter joy and the Pentecostal vision. The close of XXI rejects this potential avenue and instead returns readers to the dark world of the Prologue without Christ and *with* cardinals. The narrative follows through the effects of this subversion and rejection.

Here *Piers* shows what happens to those who are offered the sacraments but refuse to participate on its terms. "The scene, with what follows," Aers writes, "suggests that Christians now want the Eucharist only if it has absolutely no entailments for their social practices: they want Christ's gifts of the new covenant to have no consequences for their forms of life."[29] The brewer, uneducated vicar, lord, and king are diverse folk who willfully reject the life that the sacraments entail. They balk at the uncompromising moral standards of sacramental practice, preferring their more familiar habits of sin. Social, ecclesial fabric deteriorates and vices flourish. This is what happens when folks refuse to become what they receive in the sacraments. These sin-sick Christians will force the Church to make its practices more palatable.

---

28. "So Y may boldely be hoseled for Y borwe neuere / Ne craue of my comune bote as my kynde asketh" (Pearsall XIX.475–76).

29. Aers, *Sanctifying Signs*, 50.

§3 Learn to Love

In this last episode Langland traces the infectious disintegration of sin from the brewer, vicar, lord, and king to the entire community. Langland is concerned on a larger scale with the destruction of the Church at the hands of its own members. Here the Church observes sacramental practice despite their collective intention *not* to signify the unity of the mystical body of Christ the sacraments effect and the first sacrament, Christ the sanctifier.[30] The community makes its own unmaking. Everything unravels. The practices of the Church now frustrate the very virtues they are meant to cultivate and sustain. The besieged Church bears unfortunate resemblance to the subject of satire from earlier in the poem. Yet these consequences are too serious to be satirized. This final passus shows a full-scale undermining of the justice *redde quod debes* and Christ the Samaritan's work. For a Church under the rule Antichrist, the Church Herself is now *semyuief*.[31]

At the beginning of XXII, the figure of Need brings together the lessons of *semyuief* and the Samaritan about almsgiving *and* the consequences of the people's pragmatic rejection of the sacraments.[32] Personified Need begins by offering helpful insights into the legitimacy of poverty, almsgiving, and the importance of the habituation of the will through the virtue of temperance. At first blush, Need may seem trustworthy because he will both cite Christ's example and follow conventional medieval teaching that would hold that in extreme necessity all goods are common goods.[33] But soon Need goes too far. Just as the brewer, the vicar, the lord, and the king gradually empty words of their meaning, so too Need rejects the counsel of Conscience and the cardinal virtues:

---

30. ST 3.73.3: "the unity of the mystical body of Christ which is an absolute requisite for salvation."

31. Aers, *Sanctifying Signs*, 51.

32. For poverty and need throughout *Piers*, see Crassons, "Forms of Need," in *Claims of Poverty*, 21–88. The figure of Need is hotly contested. For those who regard him as a sinister and untrustworthy authority, see, e.g., Frank, "The Conclusion of *Piers Plowman*," 310–12; Adams, "Nature of Need," 273–301; Simpson, *An Introduction to the B-Text*, 232–34. Others claim that Need is a believable figure, e.g., Aers, *Community, Gender, and Individual Identity*, 62–65; Bloomfield, *Piers Plowman as a Fourteenth-Century Apocalypse*, 135–52; Kerby-Fulton, *Reformist Apocalypticism and Piers Plowman*, 146–49; Clopper, especially, argues that Need is absolutely orthodox in "Songes of Rechelesnesse", 93–97.

33 Pearsall, note to XXII.15; Aers, "Langland on the Church," 70; ST 2-2.66.7.

> So Need in great need can fend for himself
> Without counsel of Conscience or cardinal virtues,
> As long as he pursues and preserves *Spiritus temperancie*.
> For no other virtue comes close to *Spiritus temperancie*,
> Neither *Spiritus iusticie* nor *Spiritus fortitudinis*.
> . . . .
> And *Spiritus prudencie* will fail on many points. (XXII.20–24; 31)

Need corrupts the meaning of the virtues through sophistry and distortion—criticizing *Spiritus iusticie*, *Spiritus fortitudinis*, and *Spiritus iusticie*, while exalting a form of *Spiritus temperancie* above all.[34] Such temperance operates on the assumption that "Need has no law nor ever goes into debt," obviating the necessity of penance or *redde quod debes* so recently required in order to constitute the Church community (XXII.10). Although Need describes Christ as a needy figure ("Nor was there any so needy or died a poorer man" XXII.50; see XXII.35–49), the charity so recently embodied and taught by Christ the Samaritan seems remote if not irrelevant. In contrast to the people's open and overt rejection of the gifts of Grace, Need shows how this same rejection may also assume even more elusive forms that are correspondingly more difficult to discern.

Antichrist comes to reform the community by threatening *all* the cardinal virtues:

> When Need had reproached me thus, I feel asleep at once
> And dreamed quite marvelously that in man's form
> Antichrist then came, and all the top branches of Truth
> Quickly turned upside-down, and overturned the roots,
> And made falsehood spring and spread and supply men's needs;
> And in every country he came to, he cut away Truth
> And made deceit grow there as if he were a god.
> . . . .
> Antichrist thus had hundreds soon at his banner
> And Pride bore it boldly about
> With a lord that lived for the pleasure of his body,
> Who came against Conscience, who was keeper and guide
> Of all kindred Christians and cardinal virtues.
> (XXII.51–57; 69–73)

The people's systematic rejection of the demands of the virtues, the demands of *redde quod debes*, the conditions of the sacrament of penance and

---

34 See Carruthers, *Search for St. Truth*, 157–58; Mann, *Langland and Allegory*, 23, and "The Nature of Need Revisited."

of the altar, invite the leadership of Antichrist. Antichrist embodies sin and aiding the Antichrist are the seven great giants: the deadly sins.[35]

Penitential practice is a source of controversy and, in the face of the folk's persistent resistance, a catalyst for compromise. Leading the way are imperfect priests and prelates of Holy Church, followers of Antichrist on Covetousness' team (XXII.58; 220). These allies of the vices and foremost agents of corruption are of a piece with Langland's treatment of the contemporary Church throughout the poem. Here as much as anywhere one sees a Church allied with meed, with covetousness and simony, such that their identity is becoming co-extensive. Aers explains, "Both the papacy and the leaders of the English Church in the 1370s and 1380s were adamant that defending the material foundations of the Church as a major landholder and political power was an essential component in the defense of Christ's Church and Christian faith. Langland understood that this very identification of faith, Church, and the provision of temporal power as a sign of Antichrist."[36]

Conscience too is accommodated. As the poem closes, his mistakes culminate in the wide-scale destruction of the Church. At first Conscience decries the priests and prelates of Holy Church and despairs of friars "who didn't know their craft well" (XXII.231). The friars are known to be followers of Antichrist (XXII.58). But a few lines later Conscience follows the advice of Need to let the friars into Unity and Holy Church, provided that the friars "give up logic and learn how to love" (XXII.250). Envy overhears this and appeals to the friars' characteristic habits of greed—they readily forsake curing people's souls out of greed to assume university fellowships in philosophy (XXII.233; 273–95).

Conscience has Peace bolt the gates of Unity against hard assaults by Covetousness, Unkindness, and Hypocrisy (XXII.296–303). Those within Unity are wounded and sick with sin. Conscience attempts to provide sacramental salve:

> Conscience called a doctor who could give good shrift
> To salve those who were sick and wounded by sin.

---

35. Many of the figures who help Antichrist are not sinful individuals, but sinful types or personified abstractions that are evil by nature—Hypocrisy, Friar Flatterer, Sloth, proud priests, Covetousness, imperfect priests and prelates of Holy Church, the lord that lived after lust, Comfort, Pride, Fortune, Lechery, Simony, Life, Liar, Despair, Tommy Forked-Tongue. Davlin, *Place of God*, 133–34.

36. Aers, "Langland on the Church," 71. Aers adds that Langland also discredits ideologies of magisterial reformation, whether Wycliffite or sixteenth-century versions.

> Confession mixed a sharp salve and made men do penances
> For the misdeeds they had done,
> And made sure Piers' pardon was paid, *redde quod debes*.
> (XXII.304–9)

That the sin-sick need salve recalls the Samaritan and *semyuief*, yet the people are unyielding in their protest. They complain that they need a doctor who applies "softer plasters," who has a "soft touch" or "gentler treatments" (XXII.310, 313, 314)—such as Friar Flatterer.

Conscience yields.

> "Welcome," said Conscience, "can you heal the sick?
> Here's Contrition," said Conscience, "my cousin, wounded;
> Comfort him," said Conscience, "and take care of his affliction.
> The parson's plasters and powders are too painful,
>   And he leaves them on too long and is reluctant to change them;
> From Lent to Lent he lets his plasters sting."
>   "Oh, I believe that's too long," said this friar, "I'll have to correct it,"
> And goes and gropes Contrition's condition and gives him a plaster
> Made of a private payment, and "I shall pray for you
> And for those you're obliged to, all my lifetime,
> And make of you as if you're my Lady in the masses and matins
> Of friars in our fraternity for a little silver." (XXII.356–67)

Friar Flatterer's promise to correct or "amenden" (Pearsall, XXII.362) recalls the Samaritan's promise that the Father will forgive those who can "amend and repay" (XIX.201) alongside Meed's false amends (IV). The penitential practice here contrived by Friar Flatterer, Covetousness, Covetousness' team is patterned on Meed's abuse of the sacrament earlier in the poem. The sacrament of penance as *redde quod debes* is now "a plaster made of a private payment." This practice is estranged from the virtues constitutive of it and their source and sustenance: the life and work of the Samaritan in Charity.

As *Piers* ends, the salve of the sacraments becomes an enchantment, a sleeping potion (XXII.378–79). That which is meant to be a source of healing and succor for the people, "those who were sick and wounded by sin," becomes a drug which makes them "fear no sin" (XXII.305, 379). That which should be a source of conversion yields spiritual torpor. Contrition cannot come help hold the gate against Sloth and Pride, for "He lies drowned" (XXII.377).

In the last lines of the poem, Conscience becomes a pilgrim.

Two Guides for the Journey

> "By Christ," said Conscience then, "I'll become a pilgrim,
> And walk as wide as the world reaches
> To seek Piers the plowman, who might destroy Pride,
> And ensure that friars find a living, who flatter out of need
> And contradict me, Conscience. Now Kind avenge me,
> And send me good favor and health till I have Piers plowman."
> And then he cried out loud for Grace until I began to awake.
> (XXII.380–87)

Is *this* now "the way"? Conscience may seem a good fellow guide—he proclaims "By Christ, I'll become a pilgrim" to seek Piers' help. He acknowledges his own limits. He cries for Grace. But Conscience also proclaims, "Kind avenge me," a desire that is far from embodying the charitable community of forgiveness and kindness set out by the Samaritan in XIX and so recently commended by Kind in XXII.[37] Conscience loses his moral bearings. As Conscience leaves the Church so too, readers may surmise, go the cardinal virtues.

Kind orders Will to stay in Holy Church:

> "If you want revenge, make your way into Unity
> And keep yourself there till I send for you,
> And make sure you learn some craft before you come from here."
> "Counsel me, Kind," I said, "what craft's best to learn?"
> "Learn to love," said Kind, "and forget all the rest." (XXII.204–8)[38]

Will obeys Kind's command to remain with the sacraments—signs of love left for his healing and sustenance by Christ. He is charged to learn the best of crafts. The craft of love entails the practices of forgiveness and kindness embodied and explained by the Samaritan in XIX. The Church remains an eschatological community under assault by the Antichrist, whose fundamental ambivalence rests on the willing of its members.[39]

Will's journey is still not finished as the poem ends. The darkest of prospects is that Will will retain the habits of resistance exhibited thus far in

---

37. For Conscience as crucially failing to embody the insights of the preceding passus, see Deagman, "Formation of Forgiveness," 285–87, 288–89, 294.

38. Clopper also focuses on this crucial command to "lerne to louye" as "the very essence of Franciscanism" ("*Songes of Rechelesnesse*," 100). Clopper's reading requires the exaltation of the role of Need.

39. Aers puts Langland's eschatology in dialogue with other eschatological traditions in the late medieval church, including neo-Joachite strands, in "Visionary Eschatology." Aers interprets the closing of the poem as Langland's ecclesiology of the remnant in "Langland on the Church," 73–76.

the poem. He will never learn to embody the virtues because the community and practices established by the Samaritan and given to us in Grace have been transformed through accommodation to the Antichrist. This would be the fruit of the long sequence from Passus XXI–XXII where Christians willingly bring about this reality themselves by refusing the gifts of grace and commodifying sacramental practice. In this case, Christ's community can become thoroughly identical to the rest, sharing in the world's corrupt practices and unchanged agents.

Yet Will's remaining in the Church also has the potential to become a double act of edification—for himself and for the community. This fruitful act depends on coupling XIX and XXI, charity and its practices of Eucharist and penance. Will's act in staying is rooted in faith, with hope of Christ's Second Coming, undertaking the arduous task of learning to love. He lives "now in a dark manner, then face to face," and the way of going on depends *cardinally* on the work of three virtues that remain: faith, hope, and love. Through such members as Will, the Church may become a community of virtue. Its character hinges on its faithful observance of sacramental practice. At the end of the poem, these two alternatives lay before Will with two very different visions of virtue. The moral scope of the poem is, at its end, reduced to the theological virtues alone. At that, Langland names only one: love.

The virtue of which Langland writes will be cultivated only by the familiar loop from confessional, the font, and the altar and depends upon our becoming a baptismal, penitential, eucharistic people. Langland makes it clear that one may continue to retrace that loop along with holding onto our resistances, but it will mean that the sacraments appear opaque signs signifying nothing. In such a case the wayfarer can never discover the arch of his journey in the Land of Longing—the *terra longinqua*, the prodigal son's path, the land of unlikeness.[40] Such a traveler is lost in wilderness wanderings.

---

40. See Wittig, "*Piers Plowman* B, Passus IX–XII," 232–34.

Epilogue

Our Two Guides

The *Summa* and *Piers* together tell Christians that the trajectory of our journey is determined by the gift of grace *and* our own willing. In this life, one of the primary reasons the virtues remain imperfect is due to our unwillingness to become what we receive in the sacraments. We all resist the grace that would perfect us through and through, preferring our own habits of sin.

We can re-narrate what we have learned thus far concerning the virtues in light of this last revelation of the power of sin. At this point we understand the virtues better because we see *why* there are inherent limitations on our perfection in this life, *why* the will resists conversion, *why* epistemic ambiguity persists. It is at this moment that we understand *why* the way of virtue is narrow, difficult, and labyrinthine. And if we grasp all of this, then we also see *why* we are indebted to the work of fellow wayfarers Thomas and Langland—because they help us know better how to go on.

Appendix

Summary of the Action of *Piers Plowman*

PIERS BEGINS WITH A wanderer, Will, who goes into the world to hear wonders. Like everyone around him, Will hopes for great success in this world. His highest ambitions are earthly. Yet Will is not left to his own vices for long. Holy Church intervenes. She points Will beyond mere earthly goods, redirecting his path and guiding him toward a more rich conception of treasure. Will begins to desire differently as his question becomes, "How may I save my soul?" (Passus I.80). Will's question about his salvation defines his quest for the remainder of *Piers*. It turns out that "two of the surest aids to salvation, the proper employment of intellectual and material gifts, become in a fallen world the main impediments to its attainment."[1] This observation furnishes a saving thread as we follow Will along the labyrinthine path that lies ahead.

Passus I–IV begins with Will being taught by Holy Church about the proper use of the things of this world. Holy Church also shows Will her enemy, Meed. "Meed" means "due reward" in Middle English, and rewards may be good or bad. The allegorical figure of Meed is complex, and potentially dynamic, yet it seems she becomes identified with bad rewards. Her activities gradually reveal that she is immersed in this world. She happily pursues worldly success and is evangelical in persuading others to do so. She is a corrupted and corrupting influence of a piece with the societal-political-economic world. The King, Conscience, and Reason form a political

---

1. Economou, "Introduction," xvii.

alliance hoping to reform the culture dominated by Meed, but like Will they seem to have no idea of a viable way.

Passus V–IX might be said to comprise another episode or stage of Will's quest. Here the "field full of folk" are admonished by Reason to repent and seek Saint Truth for the salvation of their souls. No one knows how to repent, nor do they know "the way" to Truth (VII.158, 178). A plowman named Piers advises them to follow his map of loving God above all, preferring to die than to do any deadly sin, and loving one's neighbors (VII.205–12). But Piers overestimates their capacity to follow these directions because he underestimates the power of sin. Their guide Piers "seems to have forgotten the reason for the Samaritan's [or Christ's] journey into this land made unfit for human life, his journey to Jerusalem."[2] He forgets that grace, the sacraments, and the church are needed helps for this journey. Piers' failing becomes all the more evident in his coercive insistence that the pilgrims form a Christian community that willingly plow his half-acre—thereby reproducing the forms of domination and power characteristic of the earthly city of the preceding episode. They rebel. As Piers and a priest argue, it seems that for those under the conditions of dire poverty, who suffer at the hands of systemic injustice (and again who are without Christ and the church), outstanding questions remain regarding the status of pardon and forgiveness, how to embody the Christian counsels to perfection ("do-well"), and how to merit salvation. Will and the will make little progress along "the way" under such conditions.

Passus X–XIV comprise another stage of Will's quest. At first he roams about in search of the virtues, named do-well, do-better, and do-best. The Franciscan teachers confidently claim that the virtues stand unperturbed alongside the powerful habits of sin, but Will knows enough to remain incredulous. Abandoning his search for the virtues, deep into the "land of longing" (XI.170), the temptations of *Concupiscentia carnis*, Covetousness-of-eyes, and Pride-of-perfect living turn Will in/to Recklessness. Recklessness is duly slothful about divine things. Yet the preaching of Scripture and the parable of the marriage feast move Will to fear and trembling over his own salvation once again. He panics, grasping at the gifts of baptism without understanding the orthodox Christian understanding of all that entry into the Christian life entails—a belonging to Christ who died and rose for us, the death of sin, repentance, justification, the beginning of eternal life, becoming a member of the household of God, being subject to others and

---

2. Aers, *Salvation and Sin*, 104.

Appendix

serving them in the communion of the church, sanctification. According to Recklessness, the path to sanctification lies in patient poverty: "The poor and patient life is the most perfect of all" (XIII.99). (Passus IX–XVI comprise Langland's sustained display of Franciscan thought.) As Recklessness begins to unravel his own argument, Imaginative steps in to address some of these difficulties. Imaginative's own answers to the life of virtue subvert Recklessness' ideal of poverty and hostility to learning. Imaginative defends clergy and clerks, who would guide men of common sense to Christ's treasure. In another stab at salvation (without Christ), Imaginative seems to prescribe something like law—a law formed by culture and perhaps even amenable to Meed's lawlessness. The cumulative effect leaves Will walking "like one doomed to die," "practically out of [his] wits" (XV.1).

Passus XV to mid-XVIII constitute another middling episode in the poem. Patience is introduced as a figure who practices the ideal of mendicant poverty. Although Patience seems to be a sympathetic representation of Franciscans, she remains problematically dependent on others. She requires the vigorous activity of *Activa Vita* or Active, an apprentice of Piers the Plowman. Agricultural labor creates the necessary conditions for mendicants like Patience to crave and cry for "a square meal for a poor man, or money, if they had some" (XV.36). Moreover, Patience's poverty may lend itself to Pelagianism equally well as the active life. Patience is succeeded by Active's leader, *Liberum Arbitrium*, who identifies himself as Christ's creature. *Liberum Arbitrium* sets out to answer Will's longing: "Charity . . . that is a thing indeed / That masters praise much; where can it be found?" Will is led to the Tree of Charity, growing in a country called *Cor-hominis*, supported by the Trinity, bearing the fruit of *Caritas* as "Christ's own food" (XVIII.14). Will asks to taste of the fruit's savor, but this vision of salvation leaves Will longing for the Savior Himself. Christ is finally featured in the sequence that follows, but these re-narrations of his life are partial, with the fuller revelation yet to come.

In mid-XVIII through XIX comes that fuller revelation. Will is abandoned by *Liberum Arbitrium* and is moved outside himself to the history of the covenant. He meets Faith (Abraham) and Hope (Moses). Along with Will, they seek the final answer to questions about salvation and charity. Their character is revealed in their encounter with the Samaritan (Charity) and *semyuief* (*semivivus*, "half-alive"). This retelling of the parable displays the insufficiency of Faith and Hope alone, the identification of Will with *semyuief* in being wounded by sin and in desperate need of the help of

Appendix

Christ, and Christ's Incarnation providing the sacraments for our healing ("his body will heal us all in the end" [XIX.93]). This complex allegorical passage is, in a word, sacramental. The sacraments are medicinal, curative, and healing for the recipients, who literally cannot do anything without them. The Samaritan's salve animates a new form of life in kindness and forgiveness. The Samaritan knits together our kind (nature), kinship with Kind (God) through the Incarnation, and kindness within the community. These multiple identifications encompassing Charity/Christ display the integrity of Christian revelation at the same time as they show that *semyuief* is powerless to attain salvation on his own.

At this moment in XIX, it would seem possible for Will to see that his driving question, "How may I save my soul?" is too simple, having just witnessed this model of agency—with the wounded sinner being borne into the Church by the Samaritan. Or he might finally discern that salvation is not individual but fundamentally social. Or he might grasp that to be *semyuief* from sin entails a wound so deep that he will never embody divine charity in this life. But, despite the Samaritan teaching about and providing an example of virtue, Will does not understand what he sees.

In XX, Christ appears as the Samaritan/Piers, on his way as a knight to joust in Jerusalem. Following the Passion and Crucifixion, the Harrowing of Hell is where Christ undertakes and wins a cosmic battle. Meanwhile, the Four Daughters of God argue over how Christ will reconcile justice and mercy. Christ answers, "My righteousness and right shall reign in hell, / And mercy over all mankind before me in heaven. / For I'd be an unkind king unless I help my kin, / And namely in such need that needs to ask for help" (XX.439–42). This beautiful promise of divine forgiveness as a response to human sin, the communication of our hope for salvation, rings out in Easter joy.

Passus XXI–XXII, the concluding episode of the poem, includes the season of Pentecost and the founding of the Church. Christ bestows powers of forgiveness and mercy upon Piers, conditional upon *redde quod debes*. The failed pardon from Passus IX is christologically fulfilled, linking mercy to justice (*redde*) and confirming the social nature of salvation by rendering our dues to one another. The Spirit guides the building of the Church in elaborate agricultural allegory: Grace gives Piers the plowman a team of four great oxen (Luke, Mark, Matthew, and John), four horses (Augustine, Ambrose, Gregory, and Jerome), seeds (the cardinal virtues *Spiritus prudencie*, *Spiritus temperancie*, *Spiritus fortitudinis*, and *Spiritus iusticie*), harrowed with the Old Law and New Law, a cart (Christendom), workhorses for this cart (Contrition and Confession), and the house Unity (Holy Church).

Yet the most decisive moment of this concluding episode seems to lie instead in the unraveling of this ideal. Pride catches sight of Piers at the plow, threatening Conscience and all Christians that they would have to part with the seeds that Piers sowed (the cardinal virtues). The besieged Church responds by digging a deep ditch around Unity. The siege by sin comes from within. The people themselves balk when Conscience invites the people to Eucharist, conditional upon *redde quod debes*. They refuse to give themselves over to the life of kindness and kinship disclosed by the Samaritan and confirmed in practices of forgiveness and restitution. They willfully reject the cardinal virtues. As the bonds of unity disintegrate, Will is commanded to remain in the Church Militant with the counsel of learning the best craft: love. The conclusion of the poem returns readers to the dark world of the Prologue, yet at this late stage we readers are formed to see what we couldn't see in the Prologue. It is this: the contemporary church is ruled by the Antichrist and thoroughly assimilated to the world. The friars from all four orders "bind their love of money to their proper business" (Prologue.61) in "glossing the gospel to their own good liking" (Prologue.58), abusing the sacrament of penance (Prologue.61–64) and doling out pardons (Prologue.66–80). The target for this critique is not merely the institutions that bear out this reality but Christians themselves—for refusing to relinquish their habituation to sin, not even fearing sin, and finding themselves happy in conformity to the world's vices.

Bibliography

Adams, Robert. "Langland's Theology." In *A Companion to* Piers Plowman, edited by John Alford, 87–114. Berkeley: University of California Press, 1988.
———. "Mede and Mercede: The Evolution of Economics of Grace in the *Piers Plowman* B and C Versions." In *Medieval English Studies Presented to George Kane*, edited by Edward Donald Kennedy et al., 217–32. Wolfeboro, NH: D. S. Brewer, 1988.
———. "The Nature of Need in *Piers Plowman* XX." *Traditio* 34 (1978) 273–301.
———. "Piers's Pardon and Langland's Semi-Pelagianism." *Traditio* 39 (1983) 367–418.
Adler, Mortimer. "The Theory of Democracy—Part III (continued)." *The Thomist* 4 (1942) 286–354.
Aers, David. "Altars of Power: Reflections on Eamon Duffy's *The Stripping of the Altars*." *Literature and History* 3 (1994) 90–105.
———. *Chaucer, Langland, and the Creative Imagination*. London: Routledge and Kegan Paul, 1980.
———. "Christ's Humanity and *Piers Plowman*: Contexts and Political Implications." *Yearbook of Langland Studies* 8 (1994) 107–25.
———. "Class, Gender, Medieval Criticism and *Piers Plowman*." In *Class and Gender in Early English Literature: Intersections*, edited by Britton J. Harwood and Gillian R. Overing, 59–75. Bloomington: Indiana University Press, 1994.
———. *Community, Gender, and Individual Identity*. New York: Routledge, 1988.
———. *Faith, Ethics, and Church: Writing in England, 1360–1409*. Cambridge: D. S. Brewer, 2000.
———. "Langland on the Church and the End of the Cardinal Virtues." *Journal of Medieval and Early Modern Studies* 42 (2012) 59–81.
———. *Piers Plowman and Christian Allegory*. New York: St. Martin's, 1975.
———. *Salvation and Sin: Augustine, Langland, and Fourteenth-Century Theology*. Notre Dame: University of Notre Dame Press, 2009.
———. *Sanctifying Signs: Making Christian Tradition in Late Medieval England*. Notre Dame: University of Notre Dame Press, 2004.
———. "Visionary Eschatology: *Piers Plowman*." *Modern Theology* 16 (2000) 3–17.
Aers, David, and Lynn Staley. *Powers of the Holy: Religion, Politics, and Gender in Late Medieval English Culture*. University Park: Pennsylvania State University Press, 1996.
Aquinas, Thomas. *The Aquinas Prayer Book: The Prayers and Hymns of St. Thomas Aquinas*. Translated and edited by Robert Anderson and Johann Moser. Manchester, NH: Sophia Institute, 2000.

Bibliography

———. *Catena aurea in quatuor Evangelia, t. 1: Expositio in Matthaeum.* Edited by A. Guarenti. 2nd ed. Marietti, Taurini-Romae, 1953.

———. *Catena Aurea: Gospel of Matthew.* Translated by William Whitson. London: J. G. F. and J. Rivington, 1842.

———. *Commentary on the Gospel of Saint John.* Translated by Fabian Larcher and James A. Weisheipl. Washington, DC: Catholic University of America Press, 2010.

———. *Commentary on the Letters of Saint Paul to the Corinthians.* Translated by F. R. Larcher et al. Edited by J. Motensen and E. Alarcón. Lander, WY: Aquinas Institute for the Study of Sacred Doctrine, 2012.

———. *De veritate.* Translated by R. W. Schmidt. Chicago: Henry Regnery, 1954.

———. *Disputed Questions on the Virtues.* Edited by E. M. Atkins and Thomas Williams. Translated by E. M. Atkins. Cambridge: Cambridge University Press, 2005.

———. *Disputed Questions on Virtue* [Quaestio disputata de virtutibus in communi; Quaestio disputata de virtutibus cardinalibus]. Translated by Ralph McInerny. South Bend, IN: St. Augustine's Press, 1999.

———. *On Evil.* Translated by Richard Regan. Edited by Brian Davies. Oxford: Oxford University Press, 2003.

———. *Quaestiones disputatae.* Marietti edition. Edited by P. Bazzi et al. Vol 2. Turin: Marietti, 1965.

———. *Summa Theologiae.* In *Opera omnia.* Edited by Roberto Busa from the Leonine edition and adapted by Enrique Alarcón (Rome, 1888–1906). http://www.corpusthomisticum.org/.

———. *Summa Theologiae.* Translated by Fathers of the English Dominican Province. 5 vols. New York: Benziger, 1947–.

———. *Summa Theologiae.* Edited by Thomas Gilby et al. Blackfriars ed. 60 vols. London: Blackfriars, 1964–81.

———. *Summa Theologiae.* Translated by Alfred Freddoso. http://www3.nd.edu/~afreddos/summa-translation/TOC.htm.

Augustine. *Concerning the City of God Against the Pagans.* Translated by Henry Bettenson. Harmondsworth, UK: Penguin, 1984.

———. *De civitate Dei.* Edited by B. Dombort and A. Kalb. 5th ed. Stuttgart: Teubner, 1993.

———. *De spiritu et littera.* Corpus Scriptorum Ecclesiasticorum Latinorum 60. Turnhout: Brepols, 2005.

———. *Enchiridion.* Translated by Ernest Evans. London: SPCK, 1953.

———. *On the Morals of the Catholic Church.* Translated by Richard Stothert. In vol. 4 of *Nicene and Post-Nicene Fathers*, First Series. Edited by Philip Schaff. Grand Rapids: Eerdmans, 1989.

———. *The Trinity.* Translated by Edmund Hill. Edited by John E. Rotelle. Brookly: New City, 1991.

Baldwin, Anna P. *The Theme of Government in* Piers Plowman. Piers Plowman Studies 1. Cambridge: D. S. Brewer, 1981.

Bauerschmidt, Frederick Christian. *Holy Teaching: Introducing the Summa Theologiae of St. Thomas Aquinas.* Grand Rapids: Brazos, 2005.

Beckwith, Sarah. *Christ's Body: Identity, Culture, and Society in Late Medieval Writings.* London: Routledge, 1993.

Bennett, Josephine Waters. "The Mediaeval Loveday." *Speculum* 33 (1958) 351–70.

Bibliography

Benson, C. David. "The Langland Myth." In *William Langland's* Piers Plowman: *A Book of Essays,* edited by Kathleen M. Hewett-Smith, 83–99. New York: Routledge, 2001.

Biblia Sacra iuxta Vulgatam Clementinam. Edited by Alberto Colunga and Laurentio Turrado. 4th ed. Madrid: Biblioteca de Autores Cristianos, 1946.

Bird, Otto. "How to Read an Article of the *Summa*." *The New Scholasticism* 27 (1953) 129–59.

Bloomfield, Morton W. *Piers Plowman as a Fourteenth-Century Apocalypse*. New Brunswick: Rutgers University Press, 1962.

Blum, Lawrence. *Moral Perception and Particularity*. New York: Cambridge University Press, 1994.

Bossy, John. "The Mass as a Social Institution, 1200–1700." *Past & Present* 100 (1983) 29–61.

Boyle, Leonard. "The Fourth Lateran Council." In *The Popular Literature of Late Medieval England,* edited by Thomas Heffernan, 30–43. Knoxville: University of Tennessee Press, 1985.

———. *The Setting of the Summa theologiae of St. Thomas*. The Etienne Gilson Series 5. Toronto: Pontifical Institute of Mediaeval Studies, 1982.

Brundage, James A. *Law, Sex, and Christian Society in Medieval Europe*. Chicago: University of Chicago Press, 1987.

Burrell, David. *Analogy and Philosophical Language*. New Haven: Yale University Press, 1973.

———. *Aquinas: God and Action*. London: Routledge & Kegan Paul, 1979.

Carruthers, Mary. *The Search for St. Truth*. Evanston: Northwestern University Press, 1973.

Cessario, Romanus. "Cardinal Cajetan and His Critics." Review of *Culture and the Thomist Tradition: After Vatican II,* by Tracey Rowland. *Nova et Vetera* 3 (2005) 109–18.

———. "Is Aquinas's *Summa* Only about Grace?" In *Ordo sapientiae et amoris: image et message de Saint Thomas d'Aquin à travers les récentes études historiques, herméneutiques et doctrinales,* edited by Carlos-Josaphat Pinto de Oliveria, 197–209. Fribourg: Editions Universitaires, 1993.

———. *The Moral Virtues and Theological Ethics*. 2nd ed. Notre Dame: University of Notre Dame Press, 2009.

Clopper, Lawrence. *"Songes of Rechelesnesse": Langland and the Franciscans*. Ann Arbor: University of Michigan Press, 1997.

Coleman, Janet. *A History of Political Thought: From the Middle Ages to the Renaissance*. Malden, MA: Blackwell, 2000.

———. *Piers Plowman and the* Moderni. Rome: Edizioni di Storia e Letteratura, 1981.

Corrigan, Philip, and Derek Sayer. *The Great Arch: English State Formation*. New York: Blackwell, 1985.

Crassons, Kate. *The Claims of Poverty: Literature, Culture, and Ideology in Late Medieval England*. Notre Dame: University of Notre Dame Press, 2010.

Davies, Brian. *The Thought of Thomas Aquinas*. Oxford: Clarendon, 1992.

Davlin, Mary Clemente. *A Game of Heuene: Word Play and the Meaning of* Piers Plowman B. Cambridge: D. S. Brewer, 1989.

———. "*Kynde Knowyng* as a Major Theme in *Piers Plowman* B." *The Review of English Studies,* n.s., 22 (1971) 1–19.

———. *The Place of God in* Piers Plowman *and Medieval Art*. Burlington, VT: Ashgate, 2001.

Bibliography

———. "The Spirituality of *Piers Plowman*." In *The Mystical Gesture: Essays on Medieval and Early Modern Spiritual Culture in Honor of Mary E. Giles*, edited by Robert Boenig, 23–40. Burlington, VT: Ashgate, 2000.
Deagman, Rachael. "The Formation of Forgiveness in *Piers Plowman*." *Journal of Medieval and Early Modern Studies* 40 (2010) 273–97.
Dell'Olio, Andrew J. *Foundations of Moral Selfhood: Aquinas on Divine Goodness and the Connection of the Virtues*. New York: P. Lang, 2003.
Denzinger, Heinrich. *The Sources of Catholic Dogma*. Translated by Roy J. Deferrari from the 30th ed. of *Enchiridion Symbolorum*. St. Louis: Herder, 1957.
Di Noia, J. Augustine. "*Imago Dei—Imago Christi*: The Theological Foundations of Christian Humanism." In the *Proceedings of the International Congress on Christian Humanism in the Third Millennium: The Perspective of Thomas Aquinas, 21–25 September 2003*, 1:19–30. Vatican City: Pontificia academia sancti Thomae Aquinatis, 2004.
Dix, Gregory. *The Shape of the Liturgy*. London: Dacre, 1945.
Donaldson, E. T. *Piers Plowman: The C-Text and Its Poet*. New Haven: Yale University Press, 1949.
Duffy, Eamon. *The Stripping of the Altars: Traditional Religion in England, c. 1400–c. 1580*. 2nd ed. New Haven: Yale University Press, 1992.
Dunning, Thomas Patrick. *Piers Plowman: An Interpretation of the A-Text*. 2nd ed. Revised and edited by T. P. Dolan. New York: Oxford University Press, 1980.
Duns Scotus, John. *Duns Scotus on the Will and Morality*. Selected and translated by Allan Wolter. Washington, DC: Catholic University of America Press, 1986.
Economu, George. "Introduction." In *Piers Plowman: The C Version; A Verse Translation*, translated by George Economu, xxiii–xxix. Philadelphia: University of Pennsylvania Press, 1996.
Elders, Leo. *The Philosophical Theology of St. Thomas Aquinas*. Leiden: Brill, 1990.
Finili, Antoninus. "On the Virtue of Religion and the Infused Moral Virtues." *Dominican Studies* 3 (1950) 78–88.
Finnis, John. *Natural Law and Natural Rights*. New York: Oxford University Press, 1967.
Foot, Philippa. *Virtues and Vices—and Other Essays in Moral Philosophy*. Oxford: Oxford University Press, 2002.
Fowler, Elizabeth. *Literary Character: The Human Figure in Early English Writing*. Ithaca: Cornell University Press, 2003.
Frank, Robert. "The Conclusion of *Piers Plowman*." *Journal of English and Germanic Philology* 49 (1950) 309–16.
Galloway, Andrew. *The Penn Commentary on* Piers Plowman. Vol. 1. Philadelphia: University of Pennsylvania Press, 2006.
Garrigou-Lagrange, Reginald. *The Three Ages of the Interior Life: Prelude of Eternal Life*. Translated by M. Timothea Doyle. Vol. 1. St. Louis: Herder, 1946.
Gilson, Etienne. *The Christian Philosophy of St. Thomas Aquinas*. New York: Random House, 1956.
Gregory. *Morals on the Book of Job*. Translated by Members of the English Church. Vol. 1, Pt. 1–2. London: J. G. F. and J. Rivington, 1844.
———. *S. Gregorii Magni Moralia in Iob*. Edited by Marcus Adriaen. Turnhout: Brepols, 1979.
Griffiths, Paul. "The Limits of Narrative Theology." In *Faith and Narrative*, edited by Keith Yandell, 217–36. Oxford: Oxford University Press, 2001.

Bibliography

Harmon, Thomas. "The Sacramental Consummation of the Moral Life according to St. Thomas Aquinas." *New Blackfriars* 91 (2009) 465–80.

Hauerwas, Stanley. *Vision and Virtue*. Notre Dame: Fides, 1974.

Hauerwas, Stanley, and Sheryl Overmyer. "The Virtues of the *Summa Theologiae*." In *Working with Words: On Learning to Speak Christian*, 214–32. Eugene, OR: Cascade, 2011.

Herdt, Jennifer. *Putting on Virtue: The Legacy of the Splendid Vices*. Chicago: University of Chicago Press, 2008.

Hibbs, Thomas. "Creation, Gratitude, and Virtue." *Journal of Law, Philosophy and Culture* 3 (2009) 101–14.

———. "The Pedagogy of Law and Virtue in the *Summa Theologiae*." PhD diss., University of Notre Dame, 1987.

———. *Virtue's Splendor: Wisdom, Prudence, and the Human Good*. New York: Fordham University Press, 2001.

Hochschild, Joshua. *The Semantics of Analogy: Rereading Cajetan's De Nominum Analogia*. Notre Dame: University of Notre Dame Press, 2010.

The Holy Bible. Translated from the Latin Vulgate and diligently compared with the Hebrew, Greek and other editions in divers languages. New York: Douay Bible House, 1941.

Hugh of St. Victor. *The Two Treatises De Laude and De Amore Sponsi ad Sponsam*. Translated by a Religious of C.S.M.V. Oxford: A. R. Mowbray, 1956.

Hütter, Reinhard. "Attending to the Wisdom of God—from Effect to Cause, from Creation to God: A *relecture* of the Analogy of Being according to Thomas Aquinas." In *The Analogy of Being: Invention of the Antichrist or Wisdom of God?*, edited by Thomas Joseph White, 209–45. Grand Rapids: Eerdmans, 2011.

Inagaki, Bernard Ryosuke. "Habitus and *Natura* in Aquinas." In *Studies in Medieval Philosophy*, edited by John F. Wippel, 159–75. Washington, DC: Catholic University of America Press, 1987.

Inglis, John. "Aquinas's Replication of the Acquired Moral Virtues." *The Journal of Religious Ethics* 27 (1999) 3–27.

The International Theological Commission. "Communion and Stewardship: Human Persons Created in the Image of God." Vatican City, 2004. http://www.vatican.va/roman_curia/congregations/cfaith/cti_documents/rc_con_cfaith_doc_20040723_communion-stewardship_en.html.

Jacobs, Jonathan, and John Zeis. "The Unity of the Vices." *The Thomist* 54 (1990) 641–53.

Johnson, Mark. "An Accomplishment of the Moral Part of Aquinas's *Summa theologiae*." In *Essays in Medieval Philosophy and Theology in Memory of Walter H. Principe: Fortresses and Launching Pads*, edited by James R. Ginther and Carl N. Still, 85–104. Burlington, VT: Ashgate, 2004.

Johnstone, Brian. "The Debate on the Structure of the *Summa Theologiae* of St. Thomas Aquinas: From Chenu (1939) to Metz (1998)." In *Aquinas as Authority*, edited by Paul van Geest et al., 187–200. Leuven: Peeters, 2002.

Jordan, Mark. "Aquinas's *Summa theologiae* as Pedagogy." In *Medieval Education*, edited by Ronald Begley and Joseph W. Koterski, 133–42. New York: Fordham University Press, 2005.

———. *Rewritten Theology: Aquinas after His Readers*. Malden, MA: Blackwell, 2006.

———. "Rhetorical Form in the Historiography of Philosophy." *New Literary History* 23 (1992) 483–504.

Bibliography

———. "The *Summa*'s Reform of Moral Teaching—and Its Failures." In *Contemplating Aquinas: On the Varieties of Interpretation*, edited by Fergus Kerr, 41–54. London: SCM, 2003.

Julian of Norwich. *Showings: Authoritative Text, Contexts, Criticism*. Edited by Denise Baker. New York: Norton, 2005.

Kane, George. *Piers Plowman: The Evidence for Authorship*. 1965. Reprint, London: Bloomsbury, 2014.

Kean, Patricia. "Love, Law, and Lewte in *Piers Plowman*." *The Review of English Studies*, n.s., 15 (1964) 241–61.

Kent, Bonnie. "Habits and Virtues." In *Aquinas's Summa Theologiae: Critical Essays*, edited by Brian Davies, 223–44. Lanham, MD: Rowman & Littlefield, 2006.

———. "Moral Provincialism." *Religious Studies* 30 (1994) 269–85.

———. *Virtues of the Will: The Transformation of Ethics in the Late Thirteenth Century*. Washington, DC: Catholic University of America Press, 1995.

Kerby-Fulton, Kathryn. *Reformist Apocalypticism and Piers Plowman*. Cambridge: Cambridge University Press, 1990.

Kerr, Fergus. *After Aquinas: Versions of Thomism*. Malden, MA: Blackwell, 2002.

Kirk, Elizabeth D. "Langland's Narrative Christology." In *Art and Context in Late Medieval English Narrative: Essays in Honor of Robert Worth Frank, Jr.*, edited by Robert R. Edwards, 17–35. Rochester, NY: D. S. Brewer, 1994.

Knobel, Angela McKay. "Can the Infused and Acquired Virtues Coexist in the Christian Life?" *Studies in Christian Ethics* 23 (2010) 381–96.

———. "The Infused and Acquired Virtues in Aquinas' Moral Philosophy." PhD diss., University of Notre Dame, 2004.

———. "Prudence and Acquired Moral Virtue." *The Thomist* 69 (2005) 535–55.

———. "Relating Aquinas's Infused and Acquired Virtues: Some Problematic Texts for a Common Interpretation." *Nova et Vetera* 9 (2011) 411–31.

———. "Two Theories of Christian Virtue." *The American Catholic Philosophical Quarterly* 84 (2010) 599–618.

Langland, William. *Piers Plowman: The C Version*. Edited by George Russell and George Kane. London: Athlone, 1997.

———. *Piers Plowman: An Edition of the C-Text*. Edited by Derek Pearsall. York Medieval Texts, 2nd ser. 1978. Reprint, Exeter: University of Exeter Press, 1994, 2008.

———. *Vision of* Piers Plowman: *A Critical Edition of the B-Text Based on Trinity College Cambridge MS B.15.17*. Edited by A. V. C. Schmidt. 2nd ed. Boston: Tuttle, 1995.

———. *William Langland's* Piers Plowman: *The C Version; A Verse Translation*. Translated by George Economou. Philadelphia: University of Pennsylvania Press, 1996.

Lash, Nicholas. *Theology on the Way to Emmaus*. 1986. Reprint, Eugene, OR: Wipf & Stock, 2005.

Lees, Clare. "Gender and Exchange in *Piers Plowman*." In *Class & Gender in Early English Literature: Intersections*, edited by Britton J. Harwood and Gillian R. Overing, 112–30. Bloomington: Indiana University Press, 1994.

Lombardo, Nicholas. *The Logic of Desire: Aquinas on Emotion*. Washington, DC: Catholic University of America Press, 2001.

Long, D. Stephen, and Nancy Ruth Fox. *Calculated Futures: Theology, Ethics, and Economics*. Waco, TX: Baylor University Press, 2007.

Lottin, Odon. *Principes de morale*. Vol. 2. Louvain: Éditions de l'Abbaye du Mont César, 1947.

Bibliography

Lubac, Henri de. "*Duplex Hominis Beatitudo* (Saint Thomas 1a2ae q62 a1)." *Recherches de science religieuse* 35 (1948) 290–99; reprinted in *Communio* 35 (2008) 599–612.

Lumbreras, Peter. "Notes on the Connection of the Virtues." *The Thomist* 11 (1948) 218–40.

MacIntyre, Alasdair. *After Virtue*. 2nd ed. Notre Dame: University of Notre Dame Press, 1984.

———. *Dependent Rational Animals: Why Human Beings Need the Virtues*. Chicago: Open Court, 1999.

———. "How to Seem Virtuous without Actually Being So." Lancaster: Centre for the Study of Cultural Values, 1991. Reprinted in *Education in Morality*, edited by J. Mark Halstead and Terence H. McLaughlin, 118–31. London: Routledge, 1999.

———. "Natural Law as Subversive: The Case of Aquinas." *Journal of Medieval and Early Modern Studies* 26 (1996) 61–83.

———. "Plain Persons and Moral Philosophy: Rules, Virtues, and Goods." *American Catholic Philosophical Quarterly* 66 (1992) 3–19.

———. "Poetry as Political Philosophy: Notes on Burke and Yeats." In *On Modern Poetry: Essays Presented to Donald Davie*, edited by Vereen Bell and Laurence Lerner, 145–57. Nashville: Vanderbilt University Press, 1988.

———. *Three Rival Versions of Moral Enquiry: Encyclopaedia, Genealogy, and Tradition*. Notre Dame: University of Notre Dame Press, 1990.

———. *Whose Justice? Which Rationality?* Notre Dame: University of Notre Dame Press, 1988.

Macmurray, John. *The Form of the Personal*. Vol 1, *The Self as Agent*. New York: Harper, 1957.

Mann, Jill. *Langland and Allegory*. Morton W. Bloomfield Lectures on Medieval English Literature 2. Kalamazoo, MI: Medieval Institute Publications, 1992.

———. "The Nature of Need Revisited." *Yearbook of Langland Studies* 18 (2004) 3–29.

Marshall, Bruce. "Christ the End of Analogy." In *The Analogy of Being: Invention of the Antichrist or Wisdom of God?*, edited by Thomas Joseph White, 280–313. Grand Rapids: Eerdmans, 2011.

Mattison, William C. "Can Christians Possess the Acquired Cardinal Virtues?" *Theological Studies* 72 (2011) 558–85.

———. "Thomas' Categorizations of Virtue: Historical Background and Contemporary Significance." *The Thomist* 74 (2010) 189–235.

McCabe, Herbert. *God Still Matters*. London: Continuum, 2002.

McCue, James. "'Simul iustus et peccator' in Augustine, Aquinas, and Luther: Toward Putting the Debate in Context." *Journal of the American Academy of Religion* 48 (1980) 81–96.

McDonough, William. "*Caritas* as the *Prae-Ambulum* of All Virtue: Eberhard Schockenhoff on the Theological-Anthropological Significance and the Contemporary Interreligious Relevance of Thomas Aquinas's Teaching on the *Virtutes Morales Infusae*." *Journal of the Society of Christian Ethics* 27 (2007) 97–126.

McInerny, Ralph. "The Analogy of Virtue." http://icucourses.com/pages/004-7-the-analogy-of-virtue.

———. *Aquinas and Analogy*. Washington, DC: Catholic University of America Press, 1996.

———. "Discussion: Analogy Is Analogous." *Laval théologique et Philosophique* 22 (1966) 73–88.

Bibliography

———. *The Logic of Analogy: An Interpretation of St. Thomas*. The Hague: Martinus Nijhoff, 1971.
Miner, Robert. "Non-Aristotelian Prudence in the *Prima Secundae*." *The Thomist* 64 (2000) 401–22.
———. *Thomas Aquinas on the Passions: A Study of* Summa Theologiae *1a2ae 22–48*. New York: Cambridge University Press, 2009.
Montagnes, Bernard. *The Doctrine of the Analogy of Being according to Thomas Aquinas*. Translated by E. M. Macierowski. Edited by Andrew Tallon. Milwaukee: Marquette University Press, 2004.
Moore, R. I. *Formation of a Persecuting Society: Authority and Deviance in Western Europe, 950–1250*. 2nd ed. Malden, MA: Blackwell, 2007.
Morgan, Gerald. "The Meaning of Kind Wit, Conscience, and Reason in the First Vision of *Piers Plowman*." *Modern Philology* 84 (1987) 351–58.
Murdoch, Iris. "The Sovereignty of Good over Other Concepts." In *Virtue Ethics*, edited by Roger Crisp and Michael Slote, 99–117. New York: Oxford University Press, 1997.
Ormrod, W. Mark. *Political Life in Medieval England, 1300–1450*. London: St. Martin's, 1995.
———. "Trials of Alice Perrers." *Speculum* 83 (2008) 366–96.
Osborne, Thomas, Jr. "The Augustinianism of Thomas Aquinas's Moral Theory." *The Thomist* 67 (2003) 279–305.
———. "Perfect and Imperfect Virtues in Aquinas." *The Thomist* 71 (2007) 39–64.
Otis, Leah Lydia. *Prostitution in Medieval Society: The History of an Urban Institution in Languedoc*. Chicago: University of Chicago Press, 1985.
Pearsall, Derek. "Introduction." In *Piers Plowman: The C-Text*, edited by Derek Pearsall, 9–24. London: Edward Arnold, 1978.
Pieper, Josef. *Faith, Hope, Love*. Translated by Mary Frances McCarthy et al. San Francisco: Ignatius, 1997.
———. *Prudence*. Translated by Richard and Clara Winston. New York: Pantheon, 1959.
Pinches, Charles. *Theology and Action: After Theory in Christian Ethics*. Grand Rapids: Eerdmans, 2002.
Pinckaers, Servais. "Aquinas's Pursuit of Beatitude: From the *Commentary on the Sentences* to the *Summa Theologiae*." In *The Pinckaers Reader: Renewing Thomistic Moral Theology*, edited by John Berkman and Craig Steven Titus, translated by Mary Thomas Noble et al., 93–114. Washington, DC: Catholic University of America Press, 2005.
———. "Beatitude and the Beatitudes in Aquinas's *Summa Theologiae*." In *The Pinckaers Reader: Renewing Thomistic Moral Theology*, edited by John Berkman and Craig Steven Titus, translated by Mary Thomas Noble et al., 115–29. Washington, DC: Catholic University of America Press, 2005.
———. "Ethics and the Image of God." In *The Pinckaers Reader: Renewing Thomistic Moral Theology*, edited by John Berkman and Craig Steven Titus, translated by Mary Thomas Noble et al., 130–43. Washington, DC: Catholic University of America Press, 2005.
———. *Sources of Christian Ethics*. Translated by Mary Thomas Noble. Washington, DC: Catholic University of America Press, 1995.
Porter, Jean. *Nature as Reason: A Thomistic Theology of the Natural Law*. Grand Rapids: Eerdmans, 2004.

Bibliography

———. "The Subversion of Virtue: Acquired and Infused Virtues in the *Summa Theologiae*." *The Annual of the Society of Christian Ethics* 17 (1992) 19–41.
Potts, Timothy. *Conscience in Medieval Philosophy*. Cambridge: Cambridge University Press, 1980.
Ratzinger, Joseph. *Spirit of the Liturgy*. Translated by John Saward. San Francisco: Ignatius, 2000.
Rhonheimer, Martin. *The Perspective of the Acting Person: Essays in the Renewal of Thomistic Moral Philosophy*. Edited by William F. Murphy Jr. Washington, DC: Catholic University of America Press, 2008.
Robertson, D. W., and B. F. Huppe. *Piers Plowman and Scriptural Tradition*. Princeton: Princeton University Press, 1951.
Rocca, Gregory P. "Analogy as Judgment and Faith in God's Incomprehensibility: A Study in the Theological Epistemology of Thomas Aquinas." PhD diss., Catholic University of America, 1989.
———. *Speaking the Incomprehensible God: Thomas Aquinas on the Interplay of Positive and Negative Theology*. Washington, DC: Catholic University of America Press, 2004.
Rubin, Miri. *Corpus Christi: The Eucharist in Late Medieval Culture*. Cambridge: Cambridge University Press, 1991.
Salter, Elizabeth. "*Piers Plowman*: An Introduction." In *English and International: Studies in the Literature, Art and Patronage of Medieval England*, edited by Derek Pearsall and Nicolette Zeeman, 111–57. Cambridge: Cambridge University Press, 1988.
Scase, Wendy. *Piers Plowman and the New Anticlericalism*. Cambridge: Cambridge University Press, 1989.
Schockenhoff, Eberhard. *Bonum hominis: Die anthropologischen und theologischen Grundlagen der Tugendethik des Thomas von Aquin*. Mainz: Matthias Grünewald, 1987.
———. "Die Liebe als Freundschaft des Menschen mit Gott: Das Proprium der Caritas-Lehre des Thomas von Aquin." *Internationale katholische Zeitschrift Communio* 36 (2007) 232–46.
———. "The Theological Virtue of Charity." In *The Ethics of Aquinas*, edited by Stephen J. Pope, 244–58. Washington, DC: Georgetown University Press, 2002.
Scott, Walter. *The Lay of the Last Minstrel: A Poem*. 4th ed. London: Longman, Hurst, Rees, and Orme, 1806.
Scotus, John Duns. *Quaestiones in IV lib. Sententiarum*. Opera omnia VIII–XXI. Paris, 1893–94.
Selzer, John L. "Topical Allegory in *Piers Plowman*: Lady Meed's B-Text Debate with Conscience." *Philological Quarterly* 59 (1980) 257–67.
Shanley, Brian. "Aquinas on Pagan Virtue." *The Thomist* 63 (1999) 553–77.
———. "Aquinas's Exemplar Ethics." *Thomist* 72 (2008) 345–69.
Sherwin, Michael. "Aquinas, Augustine, and the Medieval Scholastic Crisis Concerning Charity." In *Aquinas the Augustinian*, edited by Michael Dauphinais et al., 181–204. Washington, DC: Catholic University of America Press, 2007.
———. *By Knowledge and By Love: Charity and Knowledge in the Moral Theology of St. Thomas Aquinas*. Washington, DC: Catholic University of America Press, 2005.
———. "Infused Virtue and the Effects of Acquired Vice: A Test Case for the Thomistic Theory of Infused Cardinal Virtues." *The Thomist* 73 (2009) 29–52.
Simpson, James. *Piers Plowman: An Introduction to the B-Text*. New York: Longman, 1990.
———. *Reform and Cultural Revolution*. Oxford: Oxford University Press, 2002.

Bibliography

Skeat, Walter W., ed. *The Vision of William Concerning Piers Plowman, together with Vita de Dowel, Dobet, et Dobest, secundum Wit et Resoun, by William Langland.* London: Published for the Early English Text Society, N. Trübner, 1867–77.

Smith, Ben H. *Traditional Imagery of Charity in Piers Plowman.* Paris: Mouton, 1966.

Smith, Vance. *The Book of the Incipit: Beginnings in the Fourteenth Century.* Minneapolis: University of Minnesota Press, 2001.

Sokolowski, Robert. *The God of Faith and Reason: Foundations of Christian Theology.* Notre Dame: University of Notre Dame Press, 1982.

Stump, Eleonore. "Aquinas's Account of Freedom: Intellect and Will." In *Aquinas's Summa Theologiae: Critical Essays*, edited by Brian Davies, 203–22. Lanham, MD: Rowman & Littlefield, 2006.

Suttor, Timothy. "Why Conscience Likes Dogmatic Definitions." *Canadian Journal of Theology* 14 (1968) 43–56.

Sweeney, Eileen. "From Determined Motion to Undetermined Will and Nature to Supernature in Aquinas." *Philosophical Topics* 20 (1992) 189–214.

Tawney, R. H. *Religion and the Rise of Capitalism: A Historical Study.* London: J. Murray, 1926.

Taylor, Charles. *Sources of the Self: The Making of the Modern Identity.* Cambridge: Harvard University Press, 1989.

Torrell, Jean-Pierre. "Nature et grâce chez Thomas d'Aquin." *Revue Thomiste* 101 (2001) 167–202.

———. *Saint Thomas Aquinas.* Translated by Robert Royal. 2 vols. Washington, DC: Catholic University Press, 1996–2003.

Trigg, Stephanie. "The Traffic in Medieval Women: Alice Perrers, Feminist Criticism and Piers Plowman." *The Yearbook of Langland Studies* 12 (1998) 5–29.

Vatican Council II. *Dei Verbum* (Dogmatic Constitution on Divine Revelation). In *Vatican Council II: The Conciliar and Postconciliar Documents*, edited by Austin Flannery, 1:750–65. Collegeville, MN: Liturgical Press, 1980.

———. *Gaudium et Spes* (Pastoral Constitution on the Church in the Modern World). In *Vatican Council II: The Conciliar and Posconciliar Documents*, edited by Austin Flannery, 1:903–1001. New rev. ed. Northport, NY: Costello, 1996.

Velde, Rudi A. te. *Aquinas on God: The "Divine Science" of the Summa Theologiae.* Burlington, VT: Ashgate, 2006.

———. *Participation and Substantiality in Thomas Aquinas.* Leiden: Brill, 1995.

Wadell, Paul. *Friends of God: Virtues and Gifts in Aquinas.* New York: P. Lang, 1991.

———. *Primacy of Love: An Introduction to the Ethics of Thomas Aquinas.* New York: Paulist, 1992.

Wallace, William. *The Role of Demonstration in Moral Theology: A Study of Methodology in St. Thomas Aquinas.* Washington, DC: Thomist, 1962.

Watts, John. *Henry VI and the Politics of Kingship.* Cambridge: Cambridge University Press, 1996.

Wawrykow, Joseph. "Jesus in the Moral Theology of Thomas Aquinas." *Journal of Medieval and Early Modern Studies* 42 (2012) 13–33.

Weisheipl, James. "The Principle *Omne quod movetur ab alio movetur* in Medieval Physics." *Isis* 56 (1965) 26–45.

Wetzel, James. *Augustine and the Limits of Virtue.* Cambridge: Cambridge University Press, 1992.

White, Hugh. *Nature and Salvation in* Piers Plowman. Cambridge: D. S. Brewer, 1998.

BIBLIOGRAPHY

White, Thomas Joseph, ed. *The Analogy of Being: Invention of the Antichrist or Wisdom of God?* Grand Rapids: Eerdmans, 2011.

———. Review of *Natural Desire to See God*, by Lawrence Feingold. *Thomist* 74 (2010) 461–67.

———. "The Voluntary Action of the Earthly Christ and the Necessity of the Beatific Vision." *Thomist* 69 (2005) 497–534.

Williams, A. N. *The Ground of Union: Deification in Aquinas and Palamas.* New York: Oxford University Press, 1999.

Wippel, John. *The Metaphysical Thought of Thomas Aquinas: From Finite Being to Uncreated Being.* Washington, DC: Catholic University of America Press, 2000.

Wittgenstein, Ludwig. *Philosophical Investigations.* Translated by G. E. M. Anscombe. 3rd ed. New York: Prentice Hall, 1958.

Wittig, Joseph. "*Piers Plowman* B, Passus IX–XII: Elements in the Design of the Inward Journey." *Traditio* 28 (1972) 211–80.

Wood, Rega. *Ockham on the Virtues.* West Lafayette, IN: Purdue University Press, 1997.

Yearley, Lee. *Mencius and Aquinas: Theories of Virtue and Conceptions of Courage.* Albany: State University of New York Press, 1990.

———. "The Nature-Grace Question in the Context of Fortitude." *Thomist* 35 (1971) 557–80.

Yunck, John. *The Lineage of Lady Meed: The Development of Mediaeval Venality Satire.* Notre Dame: University of Notre Dame Press, 1963.

Zeeman, Nicolette. *Piers Plowman and the Medieval Discourse of Desire.* Cambridge: Cambride University Press, 2006.

Subject Index

Aers, David, 67, 109, 111, 114
agency, 35, 46, 53, 76, 104n13
   divine–human, 81, 81n5, 86–87
   limits of, 69–70, 74
analogy, 12–34, 71, 78, 85, 88, 90–93
Aristotle, 51, 79, 83
   on the ultimate end, 18–22
Aquinas, Thomas
   on continual growth in the moral life, 1–2, 9, 11, 21, 89–90
   on the theological cast of all virtue, 8, 13, 16–18, 22–30, 78–79, 87–88, 90–91, 93–94
   Christocentrism of, 8, 13, 30–34, 93
   See also analogy; beatitude)
Augustine, 3, 5n7, 18–19, 28n59, 32, 48, 49, 58–59, 62, 67, 70, 72, 79, 79n2, 80n3, 83, 86, 88, 96, 98n5, 100, 122

beatitude
   as an analogical term, 13, 17, 18–23
   as ending in God, 11, 17–18, 20, 34, 81–83,
   as false, 28, 36, 44
   as goal of journey, 11, 22, 29–30, 35
   as imperfect/perfect, 21–22, 26–27, 29, 30, 75, 92, 94, 101
   the morality of, 12–13, 17, 23–30, 81
   as natural/supernatural, 24–29, 90, 92
   progression in, 11, 29, 82, 90
   as sharing in God's beatitude, 17, 20–22, 81–83

charity, 58, 78–94
   and community, 60–61, 71–75, 96, 98–101, 107–9, 112–13, 116, 117
   as exceeding our natural grasp, 95, 122
   as friendship, 82–83, 86, 87, 90
   as incomplete in this life, 2, 9, 78, 89–90
   as increasing in intensity, 1, 89–90
   as kindness, 61, 71–75, 97, 109, 116, 122–23
   as lacking charity, 53, 88
   to "learn to love" (PP), 2, 10, 116–17, 123
   as perfecting acquired virtues, 28, 79, 87, 89, 90–94
   as perfecting the other infused virtues, 81, 81n5, 83, 85, 86, 87
   the perfection of, 88–90
   as perfects law, 63, 65, 65n9
   as revealed in Christ, 2, 9, 59, 60, 67
   as taught by Holy Church (PP), 37, 40
   as the ultimate answer to sin, 104, 121–22
   the virtue of charity, 2, 63, 67, 71, 78–94
   See also under journey // as "the way" // of charity; Piers Plowman // Good Samaritan / Charity / Christ; sacraments // Eucharist
community
   as broken by habits of sin, 95–97, 100, 106–11, 112–13, 116

Subject Index

community *(cont.)*
  as the context for the sacraments and cultivating virtue, 2, 9, 35, 70–75, 81, 82n8, 95, 98, 116
  as corroded by market economy and Meed, 9, 42n10, 45–46, 50, 53, 56–57
  as forged in forgiveness, 73–74, 98n3, 98–99, 116
  as made perfect in Christ, 9, 60–61, 73–75, 95, 98, 116
Church, the
  as built in kindness and charity by Christ, 60–61, 73–75, 98
  as communicates the gift of the sacraments, 9, 61, 69, 71–75, 81, 95, 120
  as founded in and cultivating virtue, 2, 47–49, 98
  as marred by sin, 38, 42–43, 46–47, 49–50, 55, 95–117

delight/*delectatio*, 29, 81, 83–85, 86–87, 104
desire, 39, 61, 75–76, 116
  the formation of, 36
  as natural desire for beatitude, 18, 30, 35, 58
  the transformation of, 4, 41n8, 76, 119
  as unfulfilled, 21, 35
  as worldly, 9, 36, 39, 42, 76
Du Lubac, Henri, 25n52

forgiveness. *See* justice
Fourth Lateran Council, 17n18
friars (PP)
  as accommodated to the world, 36, 57
  the anti-fraternalism of late medieval period, 44n15
  as followers of Antichrist, 114–16, 123
  the corruption in cooperation with Meed, 44–45
friendship with God, 65n9, 81n5, 82–83, 86, 87, 90

Gaudium et Spes, 30, 34
God
  the commandment to love, 65–66
  as destiny or return, 1–2, 9, 18, 78, 81–82, 87, 89–90, 94
  the free response toward, 70, 109
  as giver of gifts or help, 18, 24, 29, 68, 74, 86, 93, 105n15
  "God works in us without us" (ST), 79–80, 94
  the human naming of God, 14–15, 17, 72
  as humans are made to the image, 30–34
  as Kindness (PP), 73, 122
  as our participation in, 1, 8–9, 20–21, 24, 61, 82, 93–94
  as primary signification of perfection terms, e.g., Virtue, 11, 13, 16, 17–18, 20–23, 25–26, 73, 82, 91
  as Trinity, 32, 34, 60, 62–63, 69–70, 72, 73
  virtue as attaining God, 1, 8–9, 11, 17–18, 22–25, 31–34, 48–49, 61, 78, 81–82, 86, 89–90
  as the ultimate end, 19–20
  See also under beatitude
grace
  the cry for grace (PP), 74
  as divine gift, 67, 75, 84, 85, 87, 93–94, 118
  as enabling, 69, 89, 93
  as habitual, 23
  as healing, 58–59, 69, 93
  from Holy Church (PP), 40
  the resistance to, 75, 96–97, 105, 108, 116, 118
  in sacraments, 2, 6, 70, 98, 112
  searching for (PP), 96, 116
  as supernatural aptitude, 27
  in virtue, 2, 33, 93–94, 98, 103
  See also under Piers Plowman
Gregory, 89, 96, 100, 102–3, 122

habit
  Aristotle on, 83, 84n14
  the development of, 29, 105
  as graced habits, 23, 89, 90
  as habitual form, 83, 87
  as kinds, 78, 84–85, 91, 112
  the perfection of, 84–90

138

Subject Index

of resistance and sin, 1–3, 6, 9, 10, 39, 57, 61, 78, 95–97, 104, 108–9, 111, 114, 116–17, 118, 120, 123
Hilary of Poitiers, 31
Hütter, Reinhard, 12–13

imago Dei
   as an analogical term, 13, 30–34
   humans to/toward God's image, 22–23, 30, 31–32
   restored in Christ, 34
infideles, 88–89

Jesus Christ, 40, 47–49, 51, 52, 56–57, 71, 73, 101, 107, 117
   as perfect virtue, moral exemplar, 2, 9, 12, 13, 18, 27, 29, 30–34, 74, 90, 97, 101
   as exemplification of charity, 2, 60, 61–71, 74–76, 105, 122
   as beginning and end of journey, 8, 11, 13, 18, 30, 81, 96
   need for, 9–10, 24, 56, 63, 67, 95, 98–99, 122
   as Image of the Father, 13, 18, 30–32
   the Incarnation, 32–34, 60, 69, 73, 81, 99n6, 120, 122
   absence of (PP), 45, 47, 52, 58, 75–77, 99, 103, 119–21
   as an answer to our deepest desires, 58
   as revealing to us our sin, 62, 77
   the gift of the sacraments, 70, 73–74, 75, 95–97, 104n12, 111, 116–17, 122
   rejection of, 108–11, 112–13, 117, 123
   See also under Piers Plowman, Samaritan // Charity // Christ
journey
   as growth in virtue, 1, 2, 8–9, 11–12, 29, 74, 81, 89–90, 117
   as possible through grace & sacraments, 6, 74, 95–96, 117, 120
   as return to God, 1, 2, 78, 87, 89–90
   as frustrated by sin, 6, 96, 114, 116, 117, 120
   as ending in beatitude, 11, 29, 81, 90
   as wandering, 35, 78, 95, 117, 119
   as beginning in faith, 81
   as sustained by hope, 81
   as continual progression, 89–90
   "land of longing" (PP), 117, 120
   as steps of love, 89
   "the way" to Truth (PP), 120
   as "the way", 2, 3, 9, 11, 58, 95, 116
   of charity, 1, 59, 60–61, 75, 78, 81, 90, 118
   of Christ's Incarnation and Passion, 81, 120
   God is beatitude's way, 82
   of new life, 58
   the other way (PP), 108
   the "right way" (PP), 81n5
   of salvation, 11
   as viable, 120
   of virtue, 1, 5–6, 78, 118
justice, 82
   the absence of, 47, 52, 57, 120
   as cardinal virtue, 48, 73, 99, 103, 104
   as made possible by Christ, 99, 103–4n12, 108, 122
   as organizing the social whole, 51, 52, 57, 99, 107, 108, 122
   as threatened by corrupt practices, 55, 56, 76, 108, 111–15, 123
   as *redde quod debes* (PP), 41, 120
   as basic definition of justice, 50, 97, 112
   as the "chief seed" (PP), 108
   as forgiveness and full restitution, 73, 75, 96, 97, 98, 99, 107, 108, 112, 113, 115, 122, 123
   as partial pardon, 57
   as site of compromise, 108, 111–15, 123
   See also law

kindness (PP), 61
   as forgiveness, 72, 74–75, 116, 122–23
   as love and charity, 73, 74, 75, 97
   unkindness, 73, 109
   See also under Piers Plowman, Kind; Piers Plowman, Unkindness

Langland, William
   action of *Piers Plowman*, 3–4; 119–23

Subject Index

Langland, William *(cont.)*
  on the Church as besieged by sin, 95–117, 122–23
  on commodification of sacraments, 44–46, 112–17, 123
  on desire being shaped by worldly treasure 39–41, 42, 109. *See also under* Piers Plowman, Meed
  on epistemic ambiguity, 1, 9, 35, 36, 75–77, 106, 109, 116–17, 118, 121
  on virtues within late medieval market economy, 35, 39, 106, 108, 111
law, 60, 62, 66, 80, 110
  as deformed by profit and the market, 9, 38, 40, 43, 46–56, 75–76, 121
  as determined by virtue, 42n9, 47, 50, 51, 58–59, 60, 63–65
  as "lavacrum-lex-dei" (PP), 68
  as law of love, 101, 103
  "Need has no law" (PP), 113
  the New Law, 47, 63, 65, 67, 96, 101, 123
  See also Piers Plowman, Law
Lombard, Peter, 83n12, 86–87
love, 37, 38, 40, 47, 51–52, 56, 59, 68, 76, 99, 101, 103, 106, 107, 117, 123
  as divine, 34, 93–94
  as exemplified in Christ, 74, 116
  forms of love, virtues as, 48–49, 94
  "if you seed love, may love be what you reap" (PP), 52
  "land of longing and love" (PP), 58
  "learn to love" (PP), 2, 114, 116
  "left it with love . . . among the four virtues" (PP), 47–49, 71
  loving and knowing God, perfection in, 34, 94
  loving God and neighbor, 65, 66
  loving meed (PP), 40, 42–43, 45, 123
  as one with kindness and charity, 73, 116
  "so that love might grow" (PP), 101
  "steps of love", 89
  See also charity; *and under* law

MacIntyre, Alasdair 7, 8n15
market economy, the, 4

practices of exchange undermining the virtues, 9, 35, 108
relationships of manipulation personified in Meed, 42, 42n10, 46, 50, 55–57. *See also under* Piers Plowman, Meed)
retreat from the world of getting and spending, 69

Piers Plowman (character personifications)
  Antichrist, 112–14, 116–17, 123
  Common Sense // Kynde Wit, 47, 54
    as founding the commonwealth, 51, 52
    as defending the Church against Pride, 106, 107
  Conscience
    as accommodated, 114–17
    as an interpreter for Will, 61
    as cooperating with the king, 52, 56, 119
    as founding the commonwealth, 51
    as identifying Piers with Christ, 76
    as objecting to Meed, 38, 42–44, 55, 100n8
    as rejected, 108, 109, 112
    as threatened, 96, 106, 123
    on the church and true virtue, 47–48
    on corrupt cardinals, 49
    on gracious offering to Christian community, 107–8, 123
    whose counsel is rejected by Need, 113
  Faith // Abraham and Hope // Moses, 59, 60, 61–65, 66, 67, 69, 77, 98, 99, 103, 121
  Grace, 50, 96–97, 100–4, 106–8, 113, 116–17, 122
  Holy Church, 36–37, 39–42, 46, 49, 52, 53, 62, 76, 96, 106, 109–11, 114, 116, 119, 123
  Imaginative, 58, 107n21, 121
  Kind, 40n6, 73, 116, 122
  Law, 55
  Liberum Arbitrium, 58, 61–62, 121

Subject Index

Meed
    as allied with False, 36, 41, 53
    as an enemy of Holy Church, 37–42, 52, 119
    as corrupting sacred and civil, 40, 42, 45, 55, 120
    as the personification of relationships within the medieval church, 46, 52–53, 76, 119
    antagonistic to law, 52–56, 64, 75–76, 121
    antagonistic to community, 56, 100n8, 119
    false amends, 73, 115
Need, 112–14
Patience, 58, 121
Piers, 50, 57, 76, 96, 98–103, 106–8, 111, 115–16, 120–23
Pride, 96, 106, 108, 110, 113, 115, 116, 123
Reason, 38, 47, 56, 64, 100n8, 119–20
Recklessness, 58, 120–21
Samaritan // Charity // Christ, 9, 59, 60–61, 66–75, 76–77, 93, 95, 98–99, 101, 103, 108, 112–17, 120–23
semyuief, 60, 66–70, 71, 74, 75, 77, 93, 95, 108, 112, 115, 121, 122
Theology, 37, 41, 45, 47, 53–54, 75–76
Tree of Charity, 58, 106n18, 121
Unkindness, 73, 114
Pinckaers, Servais, 18, 19, 24, 29
redde quod debes (PP). *See* justice

Rocca, Gregory, 15–17

sacraments, 81, 116
    the corruption of, 9–10, 44–45, 96, 106, 112–17
    as cultivating and sustaining the virtues, 2, 11, 61, 68, 72–74, 95, 118
    of Eucharist, 53, 68–71, 74–75, 96, 107–8, 111, 117, 122–23
    as forming community (*corpus Christi*), 60, 69, 70–74, 97, 98–99, 108–9, 111, 117
    as healing "salve" (PP), 9, 59, 68–69, 74, 95, 108, 114, 122
    as help along the way, 56, 95, 120
    as sustaining the journey, 6, 11, 95–96
    the demands of the sacraments, rejection of, 2, 10, 73, 77, 97, 111–12
    of penance, 39, 43n11, 44–47, 57, 68, 71, 73, 75, 108, 113, 115, 117, 123 (*see also* justice / *redde quod debes*)
    the needfulness of, 9, 75
salvation, 9, 11, 35, 39, 48, 62, 66, 67, 68, 74, 75, 76, 108, 119–22
Schockenhoff, Eberhard, 84
Sokolowski, Robert, 85
Simpson, James, 46
sin, 48, 61, 63, 67, 114
    "all that is not of faith is sin" (ST), 88
    Christ needed to reveal sin, 62–63, 74, 77, 95, 122
    Church as besieged by sin, 106–7, 112, 123
    the effects of sin, 29, 34, 58–59, 94
    as enslavement, 57, 62, 77
    as obstacle causing us to lose the way, 2, 78, 96, 104, 115
    as overlooked in corrupt Church, 45, 115
    as pressing the need for the sacraments, 66–71, 73–75, 108
    remedy in making amends, 41n8, 73
    as a second nature, 2, 74
    as undermining virtue, 9–10, 57, 96–98, 100–5, 111
    as wound, 2, 66–71, 74, 77, 93, 95, 108, 114, 115, 121
    See also habit // of resistance and sin

Te Velde, Rudi, 14–15
treasure
    as the virtues, 1
    as false, illusory, 35–37, 39, 42, 76, 119
    as true, 37, 121

virtue
    as acquired virtue, 1, 78–94, 104
    as an analogical term, 17, 23–30, 34, 71, 78, 85, 88, 90–94
    as attaining beatitude, 12, 18, 23–30, 34, 81–83, 90–94

Subject Index

virtue *(cont.)*
- as cardinal virtue, 27n53, 47–50, 71, 96–97, 98–111, 112–14, 116, 122–23
- the definition of, 18n23, 28n59, 58, 79, 83–84, 91, 94
- as do-well, do-better, do-best (PP), 57–59, 120
- as exemplar virtue, 17, 23–25, 30–34, 85, 90 (*see also* God // as primary signification of perfection terms)
- as faith and hope, 63, 67, 81, 117 (*see also* Piers Plowman // Faith // Abraham and Hope // Moses)
- as false/counterfeit virtue, 1, 28, 35–36, 47, 61, 88–89, 104–5
- as the gate of heaven, 48, 71
- as imperfect/perfect virtue, 1, 16, 21–23, 26–29, 78, 88–92, 104, 118
- as infused moral virtue or infused cardinal virtue, 10, 27n53, 80, 83–85, 97, 100–105
- as infused virtue, 1, 65, 78, 79–94, 97, 104–5
- the limits of, 9, 96, 104–5, 118
- as participation in God, 1, 15, 17, 20–21, 24, 26, 78, 82, 90
- the perfection of, 81–90, 118
- as political virtue, 23
- as theological virtue, 24–27, 59–60, 65n10, 78, 80, 85, 91, 98, 117
- as true virtue, 2, 35, 47, 61, 88, 92
- *See also* charity; journey // as "the way" // of virtue; justice; law // as determined by virtue; love // forms of virtue, virtues as *and* sacraments // as cultivating and sustaining the virtues)

Wadell, Paul, 82–83
Wawrykow, Joseph, 30n69, 33
Wittgenstein, Ludwig, 6–8

www.ingramcontent.com/pod-product-compliance
Lightning Source LLC
Chambersburg PA
CBHW022128160426
43197CB00009B/1189